S.R. Bissette's Blur
(Complete Edition)
Volume 4: Video Views
(2001-2002)

Also by Stephen R. Bissette

Aliens: Tribes
We Are Going to Eat You! The Third World Cannibal Movies
Comic Book Rebels (with Stanley Wiater)
The Monster Book: Buffy the Vampire Slayer
(with Christopher Golden, Thomas E. Sniegoski)
Prince of Stories: The Many Worlds of Neil Gaiman
(with Hank Wagner, Christopher Golden)

edited by Stephen R. Bissette
Taboo 1-9, Taboo Especial

Also from Black Coat Press:

S.R.Bissette's Blur Vol. 1
S.R. Bissette's Blur Vol. 2
S.R. Bissette's Blur Vol. 3
Teen Angels: Rick Veitch's Brat Pack and the Art, Karma and Commerce of Killing Sidekicks

edited by Stephen R. Bissette

Green Mountain Cinema I:
Green Mountain Boys

S. R. Bissette's Blur
Volume 4: Video Views (2001-2002)

by

Stephen R. Bissette

A Black Coat Press Book

S.R. Bissette's Blur (Complete Edition) Volume 4 and all its contents Copyright © 2001, 2002, 2008 Stephen R. Bissette. Cover illustration Copyright © 2008 by Stephen R. Bissette.

Cover design: Jon-Mikel Gates
Packaged by SpiderBaby Grafix & Publications.

To contact the author, please write to:
Stephen R. Bissette, PO Box 157, Windsor, VT 05089,
or visit:
www.srbissette.com

A complete set of the original *Brattleboro Reformer Arts & Entertainment* sections, featuring *Video Views* and my miscellaneous articles, and an almost-complete set of *VMag* are preserved in the Stephen R. Bissette Collection in the HUIE Library at Henderson State University in Arkadelphia, Arkansas. *The Reformer* is also accessible via microfiche at the Brooks Memorial Library in Brattleboro, VT.

Visit our website at www.blackcoatpress.com

ISBN 978-1-934543-58-0. First Printing December 2008. Published by Black Coat Press, an imprint of Hollywood Comics.com, LLC, P.O. Box 17270, Encino, CA 91416. All rights reserved. Except for review purposes, no part of this book may be reproduced or transmitted in any form or by any means, electronic or mechanical, including photocopying, recording or by any information storage and retrieval system, without permission in writing from the publisher. Printed in the United States of America.

*For Alan, Ken, Todd, Nolan and all my former comrades
and confederates in the New England Buying Group;*

We tilted a few windmills, didn't we?

Acknowledgements:

These reviews and essays were originally published in *The Brattleboro Reformer*, *VMag*, *The Chicopee Herald* and *The Reminder*. Some were also presented, in revised and expanded form, in *The Video Watchdog, Rue Morgue* and *Shock Cinema*.

Thanks, then, to my respective editors and publishers, particularly Chris Nixon (my first *Brattleboro Reformer Arts & Entertainment* editor), Willow Dannible (my second), and Jon Potter (the current *Reformer A&E* editor); Steve Murphy (*VMag* and a comrade-in-arms from my comics days/daze); Steven Puchalski (who reprinted a couple of my reviews in his excellent zine *Shock Cinema*); G. Michael Dobbs (*The Chicopee Herald*, *The Reminder*, and the dearest and closest friend of 'em all); and to Tim and Donna Lucas, who accepted expanded versions of some of these reviews for inclusion in the pages of *The Video Watchdog*, all of which are properly cited herein. Whenever possible, I have included those revised versions, as they were always superior to the *Video Views* versions, if only for the gift of a bit more time for one more polish along with Tim's invaluable editorial insights and guidance.

The previously unpublished material in this volume was written in my capacity as co-programmer of events for the Video Software Dealers Association (VSDA) and New England Buyers Group in 2002, for the VSDA "Filmmakers of Tomorrow" program; that was my final year of involvement. For a little over two years, I worked on this program with supervisor Celeste Day-

Drake, at that time the VSDA Director of Marketing and Creative Services; regards and thanks to Celeste.

Thanks to Alan Goldstein for asking me to tackle the column back in 1999. Thanks to everyone at First Run Video, including our customers. Thanks, too, to the many fellow independent video store owners, members of the New England Buying Group, and the various studio reps who provided insights, opinions, and screeners whenever necessary, and often when they weren't necessary.

Special thanks to Jon-Mikel Gates for his considerable assistance with computer and information retrieval/rescue aid provided, and for his excellent cover design work. Thanks also to Jen Vaughn and Joshua Rosen for their patient proofreading of the *Blur* volumes 3-5 manuscripts; you made a huge difference in the final product.

Thanks to then-Marjory Bleier — now Marjory Bissette — who put up with me throughout this manic two year-plus saga and opened my eyes to the pleasures of films (and life) I might otherwise have skirted. Thanks to my then-teenage offspring Maia Rose and Daniel, for the same and so much more.

Finally, thanks to Jean-Marc and Randy Lofficier, who made these collections possible.

SRB

Introduction

FOCUS & PULL

This is the final *Blur* volume collecting my *Video Views* column, which formally ended in October, 2001. The introductions to *Blur Volume 1* and 2 detail the whys, wherefores and particulars of this book series. I'll refer you to those introductions, and cease belaboring the point.

Suffice to say that the first four volumes of this book series, to the best of my abilities, archives every *Video Views* column I wrote between 1999 and 2001. A few of the following were originally published as articles, but most were the regular weekly review column. Subsequent volumes (already in the works) will similarly archive my essays and film reviews for other venues. Supplementing my digital files may, upon occasion, mean including work in later volumes that belonged, chronologically, in earlier volumes. By its conclusion, *Blur* will encompass my entire body of video review work, with the exception of horror, sf and fantasy film essays I choose to reserve for inclusion in the upcoming *Gooseflesh* volumes. With a few exceptions, those concerning regional filmmakers are archived in the *Green Mountain Cinema* book series (Volume 1 now available from Black Coat Press).

The Brattleboro Reformer was my regular weekly publisher. The *Video Views* columns began in the *Reformer*'s *Arts & Entertainment* (hereafter *A&E*) on September 9, 1999, and continued weekly thereafter through October of 2001. I never missed a deadline. *Blur, Vo-*

lume 1 collected every *Reformer Video View* column from that first entry to March 30, 2000; *Volume 2* collected the *Video View* columns from April to the end of October, 2000, and *Volume 3* brought the archiving up to May 2001. This collection continues that chronology, beginning in May 2001 and concluding with my final *Video Views* columns of October, 2001, incorporating various reviews and/or film-related articles written and/or published in other venues between 1999-2002. You'll notice a different orientation from the first entries collected in this volume, including the weekly 'Short Cuts' cappers.

Blur, Volume 1 incorporated capsule reviews written for the Northampton, MA based free monthly zine *VMag* (which debuted November 1997), edited and published by my friend Stephen Murphy.[1] Those capsule reviews in fact led to my writing the weekly *Video Views* columns for The *Brattleboro Reformer*. As noted in *Blur Vol. 3*, my final *Video Views* review appeared in *VMag* in March 2001; I'd decided at that point to cease submitting reviews thereafter, but it was a moot point, as that very issue proved to be *VMag*'s *final* issue.[2]

For the record, my editor at the *Reformer A&E* in the home stretch was Jon Potter. Through no fault of Jon's, I chose to terminate *Video Views*; by the time I

---

[1] Despite my best efforts, the lack of original digital files and/or a complete set of *VMag* (neither I nor Steve Murphy have yet found a copy of the November 2000 issue) means a definitive inventory of my *VMag* work remains inconclusive at this writing. In the unlikely event that further *VMag "Video Views"* material surfaces, I will incorporate it into future volumes of *Blur* for the sake of completion.

[2] See *Blur, Vol. 1*, pp. 22-23.

departed, another local writer named Nathan Hurlbut was writing film reviews on a weekly basis, too, so I don't even think I was missed. I found that the *Reformer* was publishing my column online, *sans* permission or payment. About the same time, the *Reformer* changed editors and corporate ownership. Coincidentally, the same week I was going to request *The Reformer* to pay me a bit more for the column if they intended to publish *Video Views* online, Jon had been instructed to cut back *Video Views* to running biweekly rather than weekly, ostensibly as a cost-saving measure (I was being paid the princely sum of $25-50 per column; note that all that had made it affordable to continue *Video Views* was the fact that my employer First Run Video matched the *Reformer*'s modest weekly payment). Given that news, it was easy to walk away.

Jon invited me to continue writing for the *A&E* section, and I occasionally did so for the next three and a half years – almost exclusively about local and Vermont films and filmmakers – until the *Reformer* published my two-part article on the first Center for Digital Arts student feature, *Collie Rottweiler and the Hangaround Kid* (2005) in May, 2005. After I invoiced Jon, per usual, the new corporate owners of the *Reformer* sent me a letter and attached contract requiring, sans negotiation or additional payment, that I retroactively sign away all rights to the writing I'd done for the *Reformer* – further informing me that I would not be paid for the published *Collie* piece until I signed.[3] I refused, was never paid for

---

[3] My essay on that experience will grace the pages of the forthcoming *On/In Comics, Volume 1*, from Black Coat Press. I have not included the post-*Video Views* articles in *Blur*, saving them for a future volume of *Green Mountain Cinema*.

that last published article (funds I was going to donate to the Center for Digital Art, per arrangement with the CDA), and, expressing my regrets to Jon Potter, ceased writing for the *Reformer* for good.

Prior to that, though, it had been a good run. As noted in the previous trio of volumes, the *Reformer* was not the only home for *Video Views*. My good friend G. Michael Dobbs also occasionally published my column in his Massachusetts weeklies, *The Chicopee Herald* and *The Reminder*.[4]

The body of work showcased in this volume has one more source that must be gratefully acknowledged. By the winter of 2000-2001, more and more of my columns were being revised and expanded for publication in *The Video Watchdog*, edited and published by my good friends Tim and Donna Lucas. Whenever possible, I have included those revised versions herein, as they were always superior to the *Video Views* versions, if only for the gift of a bit more time for one more polish, and Tim's invaluable editorial insights and guidance. Thank you, Tim, and long may the *Watchdog* bark.

A few of the reviews collected herein were also submitted to *Shock Cinema* – among the best of the remaining film fanzines, and I'm still a faithful subscriber – though only a couple were ultimately published. I also had a curious submission dance with the popular Canadian newsstand horror magazine *Rue Morgue*, which treated me abominably over the submission of just two

---

[4] Again, records of what reviews were published when and where in Mike's newspapers are sketchy; despite Mike's best efforts, not every published piece was archived in my own files, and neither of us kept proper records. I've no idea if any of this final run of Video Views saw print in Mike's papers.

short reviews (one of which – included herein – was sent as a *sample* of my work; the editor published it, *sans* comp copies or payment of any kind). The funny thing was, the *Rue Morgue* editor involved didn't see anything wrong with what happened, which made it easy to walk away from that mess.[5]

With all this walking away, clearly, the writing was on the wall: it was time to end this phase in my career and move on to something more productive (thankfully, The Center for Cartoon Studies opened its doors in the summer of 2005 and invited me in from the start, and I'm happily working there to this day; more on that in moment).

As to the *Blur* format:

The dates given before each column cite the original date of publication in the *Reformer*; all other publishing venues are appropriately footnoted. On those occasions when unforeseen editorial decisions resulted in a column being 'bumped' to the following week or otherwise revised, I have preserved the chronology in which the columns were written (corresponding, by and large, with the respective video release dates), incorporating editorial alterations only when they improved or significantly altered the context of the published review. Longer columns were sometimes run as two-part pieces; those columns are specified as such with their respective publication dates, and annotated as necessary. As *Video Views* grew and reader response proved favorable, my editors seemed happy to indulge even my wildest schemes until that fateful fall of 2001. I have also cross-referenced reviews published in *Blur, Volume 1-3*, and

---

[5] My essay on *this* experience will also grace the pages of the forthcoming *On/In Comics, Volume 1*, from Black Coat Press.

footnoted updates on the filmmakers interviewed for the *Video Views* columns in this volume.

Unlike my ongoing writing for the horror film fan magazines (which will be collected in the book series *Gooseflesh*, also from Black Coat Press), I could not presume my readers knew anything about films or filmmakers. There was no communal shorthand I could rely upon. I was writing for an audience that *might* know who Alfred Hitchcock, Steven Spielberg, and George Lucas were, but maybe not. For most *Reformer* readers, only the big movie stars had any name value or instantly-identifiable celebrity. So I took it upon myself to remind readers in almost every column that individuals, artists, indeed made these movies, these videos, that filled the new release wall at First Run Video. I hoped to elevate the interest level in the medium by doing much more than write capsule reviews, but in doing so always had to be sure I provided constant reference points. Thus, I would cite other works by the same filmmakers, other films performers had appeared in, specify cinematic precursors and sources.

In the disposable forum of a weekly newspaper column, this wasn't intrusive, but once those columns are collected, the repetition of certain filmographies or references can seem rather dreary. Still, I have decided to run the columns as they originally were published. This may make these collections more useful for younger readers and neophyte film buffs, but I hope this aspect of the columns collected in this series won't prove too exasperating to the knowledgeable film aficionados who deign to dig into these writings.

Another aspect of *Blur* I should explain is that *Video Views* reflected of my working days and nights in the video industry, specifically my work with First Run

Video and the New England Buying Group during this period. It is manifest in these columns, and provides a record of sorts of those years in a form that's digestable and (hopefully) entertaining to read.

The most curious aspect of this period for me personally was the disconnect many comics peers, professionals and fans expressed, not only over my 1999 retirement from the American comics industry, but over my working in the video industry – specifically, working at a mere video store (the 'superstore' First Run Video). Mind you, I was quite happy with this change in professions (the comics industry had become a completely toxic environment for me by 1998-99), providing me as it did with a job, a haven, steady income and access to a medium (cinema) I love as much as comics. To me, a major obstacle (how to continue earning an adequate living in comics) opened up into a major opportunity, though folks in comics didn't ever see it that way. I might as well have been digging ditches or working at a sewage treatment plant as far as they were concerned – *or worse*. There was a presumption that it was only a blue-collar job, after all – though in reality, working at First Run Video ended up plugging me into another vast creative community, and teaching me about mercantile issues I'd never grasped – and a rather arrogant presumption, too, that somehow the comics community was 'better' than anything I might find elsewhere. Nothing could have been further from the truth.

At times this disconnect was a source of great concern and even distress to others. My favorite encounter (back in November of 2000) involved a shaggy black-haired teenage lad who was a First Run Video customer. He glared intently at me and literally staggered out of the store upon finding out I was 'the' Steve Bissette; clearly, my working at First Run was a major upset from whatever his image had been of me. A week later, friends steered me to a Grant Morrison website or discussion board (in any case, Morrison was the moderator) where a Morrison fan posted that he'd seen me working in a video store and noting with some disgust my writing video reviews for the local paper,[6] candidly expressing his disbelief and a sense of horror.

Morrison's reply – that he'd rather kill himself than subjugate himself to such an ignoble fate – was fairly representative of a shared view in the comics industry at the time.

Having fought many of the trench battles at DC Comics in the 1980s that afforded the realignment of fairer treatment, income, and opportunities for the next generation of creators – Grant Morrison included – I could only thank my lucky stars I had found gainful employ away from the work-for-hire plantations that had so completely reclaimed the remnants of the comics market after the 1996-97 implosion of the Direct Sales market. For me, the implosion of not only the market but the community I'd once felt part of was a source of some anger and disgust; given the revolutionary fervor I'd once shared with former friends and allies in the comics community, it was, at times, a bit like living out portions of *Animal Farm*. Though it was initially difficult to shift gears – like most American males, I confused what I *did* for a living for who I *am* – I was glad to be free and rid of it. The life-change was good for me in the short and

---

[6] This young Morrison fan specifically cited my review of *The Gladiator*; see *Blur, Vol. 3*, pp. 40-45; to him, my writing *Video Views* for the local newspaper was another symptom of how 'the mighty had fallen,' if you will.

long term, opening up new doors and whole new worlds, and I'm forever grateful it happened and that I was up to the challenges involved. I had and harbor no regrets.

From the beginning, I was treated much better and with more professional courtesy and mutual respect in the video industry than I ever had experienced in the comics or magazine industry. In fact, working in the video industry got me through what would have otherwise been some rocky years financially and allowed me to responsibly see through my two children's teenage years (and my divorce from my first wife). This sea change also brought me into the video industry at a time when that marketplace was suffering upheavals much like those the direct-sales comicbook market had barely survived in the mid-1990s. The issues were surprisingly similar, as were the industry dynamics, though they played out on a far vaster scale in the video industry. I found myself of real value here, useful to the new community I was plugging into daily – and that, too, was revitalizing.

For a stretch, I was the right person in the right place at the right time – my prior first-hand experiences served my employer and fellow video retailers rather well from 1999-2001. There were times when I found fate dealing me some pretty lively hands which my decades in the comicbook industry had unexpectedly prepared me for, including some closed-door sessions with studio representatives involving petty abuses of raw power unlike any I'd witnessed or experienced in comics (I discuss this at some length in the introduction to *Blur Volume 2*, and refer you to that volume).

Best of all, thanks to my First Run Video years, I made many lasting friendships among the independent filmmaking community. What had begun with some pleasant bar conversations at video trade shows and a couple of guest appearances of filmmakers at our Brattleboro, Vermont video superstore (directors Jay Craven, Nora Jacobson, Stefan Avalos, and Lance Weiler[7]) grew into increasing active contact with eager, hungry and very creative independent filmmakers seeking bridges to eager, hungry and very creative independent retailers. I was more than happy to lend a hand, building upon my personal experiences as a publisher and self-publisher who'd worked hard during my years in comics to construct similar ties with independent comics retailers.

My involvement with the Video Software Dealers Association (VSDA) and their initial "Filmmakers of Tomorrow" program (initiated in part by *The Last Broadcast* co-director Lance Weiler) led to often mutually rewarding interaction with filmmakers whose work I gravitated to, and which we chose to carry in First Run Video. By 2000, this made me a 'person of interest' to the VSDA, too, though they never quite seemed to grasp there was no vast untapped revenue stream to be siphoned from (independent filmmakers, like independent self-publishing cartoonists, are rarely rolling in the dough). Thanks to these exchanges, I also met many other filmmakers, including Mark Tapio Kines, Rich Mauro, and Vince Mola, and forged lasting friendships with a few, such as Lance Weiler and Stefan Avalos. I only wish I could have done more bridge building. For a time, this proved productive for everyone involved, and it's a pleasure to at last archive those efforts herein.

This new community also reawakened my lifelong interest in regional films and filmmakers, prompting me to research my home state's cinematic legacy and nur-

---

[7] See *Blur, Volume 1* and *Green Mountain Cinema I*.

ture relations with local filmmakers, if only to savor their work and record, whenever possible, interviews with them about their films and creative lives. This led to lasting friendships with marvelous people and artists like Walter Ungerer, Nora Jacobson, Alan Dater, Lisa Merton, John Douglas, Andy Reichsman and many others.[8]

Another unusual dividend of these budding relationships, thanks to filmmaker Nora Jacobson (*My Mother's Early Lovers*), was rekindling one of my oldest lifelong relationships with my Waterbury Center, VT friend and former high-school classmate George Woodard. Thanks to Nora's personal appearance at First Run Video with her film's co-star – George – accompanying her, George and I picked up our friendship after 25 years apart. This has been a real joy and pleasure, and it never would have happened had I not gone with the flow and engaged with my new life path in the video industry.

That all said, *Video Views* was also a lifeline: my one regular creative outlet that bought a bit of time to write. It didn't matter much to me what I was writing about – it all interested me, some of it passionately, and yielded a weekly column that enjoyed an audience that responded, often face to face in conversation, with energizing intelligence and immediacy. It also instilled a discipline I'd rarely enjoyed as an artist, and an orientation to writing – as a process, a pleasure and a daily exercise – that has served me well ever since.

My employment at First Run Video was a good run, overall. We even won the coveted VSDA Retailer of the Year Award for Independent or Small Chain Video Sto-

---

[8] See *Green Mountain Cinema I* from Black Coat Press; more books on Vermont films and filmmakers are in the works.

ries in July 2002; I was with Alan Goldstein at the VSDA trade show at the Las Vegas, NV Rio Suites Hotel & Casino to accept it.[9] My employment as co-manager and buyer at First Run ended on the week of my birthday, March 2005. I recently stumbled on this archived text I'd posted on my website:[10]

As of this week, I am no longer at First Run Video. I have been a partner in the business since it opened in November of 1991, and worked there full-time from 1998-2004, and remained active as a buyer for the store and a participant in First Run's activities with the New England Buying Group until this past week. It's been a lively few years: I've played a part in bringing many indie videos into our area. I've aggressively campaigned for our buying group to pick up worthy titles deserving of special attention (such as The Last Broadcast, *the first all-digital theatrical feature), films that distributors have ignored or rejected (Mark Borchardt's curio* Coven, *the subject of the documentary* American Movie, *and others), and regionally-produced features of special interest to our customer base (including Jay Craven's* A Stranger in the Kingdom, *Rusty DeWees'* The Logger, *parts one and two, and Nora Jacobson's excellent first narrative feature* My Mother's Early Lovers). *Over the years,*

---

[9] See *Brattleboro Town Crier*, Vol. 42, No. 51, Friday, August 16, 2002, pg. 1, which also sports a photo of yours truly and Alan accepting the award from VSDA National Chairman of the Board Tom Warren; a copy of this newspaper resides in the Bissette Collection at HUIE Library, Henderson State University, Arkadelphia, Arkansas.

[10] March 18, 2001, http://www.comicon.com/bissette home page.

we sponsored numerous filmmaker appearances at First Run and other NEBG member stores to call special attention to not only their films, but all independent films most casual renters idly pass by en route to the latest big-budget, major studio "flavor of the week" new release. By doing so, we set our stores apart from the video chains, sparked consumer interest in a wider diversity of options and alternatives, and reaped the benefits (monetary and karmic) of cultivating fresh pastures in our respective communities.

Though I know these projects are of peripheral interest at best to most comicon.com visitors, you should know my efforts to nurture the independent film scene (and build bridges between indy creators and merchants in the video market) have led to my own creative endeavors in the field, already underway. For years, I was as passionate about building these 'indy bridges' between filmmakers and retailers as I once was in the independent comics and self-publishing scene. Consolidation of corporate power has taken a terrible toll on indy video on both the creative and mercantile sides of the fence – much as similar forces crushed the direct comics market in the late 1990s. Though I'm no longer there, First Run is still alive and kicking,[11] though, and will be for years to come. Support your local video store (if there's one left anywhere in driving distance around you)! If you're only renting major Hollywood films from your local Blockbuster, you have no idea what you're missing.

By the time I departed First Run, the indie video retailers I felt the greatest kinship with had either closed

---

[11] First Run Video is still open and doing business as of this writing in August, 2008.

their doors, died (I kid you not), or were circling their wagons as best they could for a new round of legal scraps and business strategies dealing with the monolithic forces of the corporate studios and chains. I'd played my part as best I could – a role that included the weekly *Video Views* column, which (thanks to the reprints in *VMag* and Mike Dobbs's weeklies) also served some of the Massachusetts video shops in the New England Buying Group – and it was time to move on.

Thankfully, the Center for Cartoon Studies needed me, and it was an appropriate time for me to re-engage with my creative life in a manner that allowed me to share my skills and knowledge with a new generation of creative individuals.

As with all things in life, one's path bears unexpected riches and fruit. My time in the video industry has made me a better teacher; my experience as a merchant and retailer taught me volumes I wish I'd known as a self-publisher. My time writing has made me a better artist; the path (including *Video Views*) that led from my sadly tabling my beloved *Tyrant* (my self-published comics series, the culmination of all I'd worked for in comics) to my joining the joyful new community at CCS has prepared me for this new experience in ways I otherwise would not have been prepared.

I wish I could have said that to the shaggy teen lad who found it so appalling that I was working in a video store, writing *Video Views* for the local newspaper – well, he was young. He'll learn. Maybe he'll even read this one day.[12]

Central to my new life at CCS and this ongoing teaching and sharing process is the weekly CCS Movie

---

[12] Grant Morrison, on the other hand, should've known better.

Club film classes with the students, which quite directly builds on the lifelong calling I articulated in the intro to *Blur Volume 1* and all that's reflected in these pages.

None of it is time wasted to me, and I'm glad to have the means at last (thanks to Black Coat Press) to showcase this forgotten body of work.

As I've said every volume's introduction – it's a blur no longer.

I hope that is now true for you, too.

Enjoy.

2001

May 17:

HOME TO TIBET: This truly magnificent, profoundly moving documentary by Marlboro Productions' own Alan Dater and Lisa Merton is the definite pick of the spring video crop, and not to be missed.

For almost two decades, Alan (beginning with *A Love of the Land*, 1976, and his collaborative work on the rarely-screened *The Stuff of Dreams,* 1978) and Lisa (working with Dater throughout the 1990s) have forged a distinctive body of work bridging localized and international issues via intimate portraits of individuals. *Home to Tibet* (1996, but brand new to the video rental market) is undoubtably their most expansive and well-known work, having played across the country and around the world for half-a-decade – it just played theatrically in Hanover, NH and is currently screening in Basil, Switzerland – and its allure is irresistible. But all of Alan and Lisa's recent work (including *Learning to Trust*, 1999, and *The World in Claire's Classroom*, 2000) share the thematic anchor of how people and communities can, must, and do interact with the world at large.

In a mere hour, the filmmakers usher us into the transformative 1993 sojourn of local Greenfield, Massachusetts stonemason Sonam Lama, who braved possible incarceration to return to Chinese-occupied Tibet. Lama had fled with two companions twelve years before; having since established his American citizenship, Sonam sought contact with his homeland and surviving family, bringing with him the blessings of His Holiness the Dalai Lama and the hope of escape from, and new life outside of, Tibet.

Dater, too, risked much to accompany Sonam on his journey home, and his camera succinctly captures the existence Sonam once fled. Under Chinese rule since 1949, Sonam's people have been denied their culture, heritage, and fundamental dignity. Relegated to the role of sub-citizens in their own country, Tibetans who remain in Tibet scrape out meager livings shorn of their cultural and religious roots: education is discouraged, as is devotion to Buddhism and the Dalai Lama, while poverty, alcoholism, disease, prostitution, starvation, and crime is rampant.

Sonam's pilgrimage through these straits culminates in a heartbreaking reunion with his sister Karma, at which point the film's voice-over narration gives way to subtitled dialogue between Sonam and his family. A plan for Sonam to shepherd his fourteen-year-old niece Yangchen and eight-year-old cousin Lhamo out of Tibet for a new life in India takes shape, and *Home to Tibet* moves toward its stirring conclusion.

Many find the sheer scope of international issues (such as the Chinese rule and repression of Tibet) difficult to engage with: they seem too enormous, too exotic, too geographically apart from our own day-to-day lives. It is impossible to maintain such cultured distance and apathy once the toll of such institutionalized repression is communicated in such intimate terms: in the end, these parents and children, so much like ourselves and our own, embrace probable lifelong separation so that the children might be educated (a standard of life here so many of us take for granted). Alan and Lisa humanize political issues and arenas by opening our eyes and hearts to the lives of their subjects, and few films of any kind do so with the power of *Home to Tibet*. This is a remarkable work, vital, essential, and alive, and we are fortunate to finally have it available for rental and sale on home video. Highest recommendation! *(Unrated, but suitable – and recommended – for all ages.)*

SHORT CUTS (Recent & Recommended):

ALL THE PRETTY HORSES: Visually exquisite adaptation of Cormac McCarthy's bestseller from director Billy Bob Thornton (*Sling Blade*, 1996) finds Texan cowpokes Matt Damon, Henry Thomas, and Lucas Black coming of age south of the Rio Grande. Shifty drifter Black reclaims property, dreamy Damon courts the lovely Penelope Cruz, and loyal Thomas tags along – and all face the music in this truncated coming-of-age western. Beautifully filmed and nicely underplayed, but a little light in the saddle: Thornton's original cut was shorn by half, leaving this episodic but evocative skeleton of an epic to join the ranks of Marlon Brando's *One-Eyed Jacks* (1961) and other *"coulda been, shoulda been"* halfbreeds. Sadly, Columbia Tristar's DVD offers the same theatrical cut as the video, but it sure is purty. *(Rated 'PG-13' for violence, nudity, adult and mature content.)*

BEST IN SHOW: The latest offbeat 'mockumentary' confection from Christopher Guest (*Waiting for Guffman*, 1996) and *Second City* vet Eugene Levy lovingly follows a diverse cast of dog-lovers to Philadelphia's annual Mayflower Dog Show, converging to compete for the coveted blue ribbon. Guest scores here as the driest of the dry amusements on the floor as bloodhound aficionado Harlan Pepper amid a stellar improvising cast. Levy teams with Norwich terrier co-owner Catherine O'Hara, hair-salon proprietors Michael McKean and John Michael Higgins snuggle over their Shih Tzu, yuppie neurotics Parker Posey and Michael Hitchcock obsess over their canine 'child,' and trophy wife Jennifer Coolidge bonds with handler Jane Lynch for their prize-winning poodle, but they all take a back seat to the devastating non-chemistry between show 'anchors' Fred Willard and Jim Piddock. If Guest's trademark leisurely pace and affection for eccentrics isn't your cup of tea, stay with it for Willard, who wins Best in Show hands down. *(Rated 'PG-13' for language, some sexual innuendoes.)*

INCUBUS: Here's a real oddity: William Shatner stars in the only feature ever made in the invented language Esperanto, a long-lost 1965 curio written and directed by Leslie Stevens (don't fret, it's subtitled in English). The single surviving print was recently uncovered by producer Anthony Taylor in France, and this restored, subtitled video and DVD release is a revelation. Completed in the wake of Stevens' tenure as co-creator, producer, and frequent writer-director for the original TV series *The Outer Limits* (1963-65), this marvelous, mystical film unreels like a timeless folk tale as two demon sisters plot to drive an honorable man (Shatner) to damnation. When one of the sisters falls in love with the mortal, the other conjures the titular male demon from hell itself to bring the man down. Stevens wisely engaged his *Outer Limits* creative ensemble, including cinematographers Conrad Hall (who scored an Oscar just last year for *American Beauty*) and William Fraker and composer Dominic Frontier. The result is pure black magic, a resurrected cinematic gem. The DVD (featuring commentary and interviews with star Shatner, producer Taylor, and cinematographers Hall and Fraker) is particularly recommended. *(Unrated, but most likely falls into 'PG-13' turf for occult imagery, adult and mature situations, and tastefully handled sexual content.)*

And don't forget the best of the rest: ***ALMOST FAMOUS*** (Cameron Crowe's 1970s autobiographical rock'n'roll gem), ***BELLYFRUIT*** (a great drama about a trio of unwed teen mothers), ***BILLY ELLIOT*** (coalminer's son finds his true path dancing ballet), ***DANCER IN THE DARK*** (Lars Von Trier's moving, harrowing mutant musical starring Bjork), ***DRIVEN*** (1996, not the theatrical Sly Stallone actioner, but sober, meditative portrait of L.A. cabdrivers on the fringe), ***THE EMPEROR'S NEW GROOVE*** (lively, entertaining Disney animated feature is atypical and best of the studio's recent efforts), ***FINDING FORRESTER*** (Gus Van Sant's latest halls-of-academia parable), ***HAMLET*** (great contemporary version of Shakespeare's classic set in modern corporate NYC), ***QUILLS*** (Geoffrey Rush is the Marquis de Sade in Phil Kaufman's excellent, adult drama), ***REMEMBER THE TITANS*** (stirring anti-segregation football drama with Denzel Washington leading solid cast), ***TIGERLAND*** (riveting Vietnam War-era tale of sharp Texan loner recruit vs. the military), and ***THE WONDER BOYS*** (top-drawer cast soars in fine, funny snapshot of college prof Michael Douglas in a downward spiral). Recommended, one and all!

May 28: GOING HOME: Alan Dater, Lisa Merton Discuss **Home to Tibet**

Looking out from the porch of Alan Dater and Lisa Merton's Marlboro home on a beautiful spring morning, one could almost forget all is not right with the world... or that there even is a world beyond.

This morning, we're talking about one of the more exotic and troubled corners of that world beyond – and their film *Home to Tibet*, which just made its home video rental debut.. Alan notes that the film has not dated since it was filmed in 1993. *"If anything, things are worse there now than they were then,"* he says, *"The importance of the message is still vital, which is sad... but at least the film still has a use."*

Lisa notes how closely the plight of the Tibetan people resembles that of the Native American nations. Under Chinese rule since 1949, Tibetans have been denied their culture, heritage, and fundamental dignity as a people. Education is discouraged, as is devotion to Buddhism and his holiness the Dalai Lama, while poverty, alcoholism, disease, prostitution, starvation, and crime is rampant. But Lisa also notes that *Home to Tibet* is not in and of itself condemning China: *"It is not the Chinese people who have strangled Tibet: it's the government. You really need to distinguish between the two – in most countries, you need to distinguish between the two, but there you really need to. There are a lot of Chinese who have experienced the same kind of repression the Tibetans have."*

In this Marlboro backwoods haven, expression, not repression, is vital. Alan and Lisa have maintained ongoing links with friends, associates, and acquaintances around the globe. In their Marlboro Productions studio, they continue to sculpt passages of time (recorded onto film and/or videotape) into coherent, often profoundly moving portraits of people and communities interacting with the world at large. Those films are their link with the planet; through them, Alan and Lisa communicate their shared perceptions, and thus interact with – and change – the world.

Their work also shapes and changes them: *"It changed us,"* Lisa says of *Home to Tibet*, *"having this connection with Sonam* [the subject of the film], *and now we're connected to his family and this whole Tibetan world that we're very much a part of. It's something that we'll always be part of, and that will always be part of us."*

The bedrock for Alan and Lisa's work was laid with Alan's early collaborative documentary efforts, including *A Love of the Land* (1976), *The Stuff of Dreams* (1978), and intimate portraits of local artists in *Blanche* (1987), *Wolf Kahn: Landscape Painter* (1990), *Bridge of Fire* (1991), and *Michelle Holzapfel* (1993). Kindling their personal and professional relationship throughout the 1990s, Lisa and Alan stretched beyond this regionalized canvas to create their most expansive work, *Home to Tibet* (1996).

They've since built upon that accomplishment with *Learning to Trust* (1999), showcasing an intensive conflict resolution workshop filmed at the School for International Training, and *The World in Claire's Classroom* (2000), exploring how veteran Westminster West teacher, VT teacher Claire Oglesby opens the eyes of her first and second grade classes to local and international community issues. They are currently investigating a possible project about White River Junction's V.A. hospital, while working on a film about Vermont ceramic potter Karen Karnes.

Still, *Home to Tibet* continues to touch new audiences. *"It keeps getting people involved,"* Lisa says, *"and informing people about something most of us don't know anything about."*

Home to Tibet chronicles the 1993 journey of Greenfield, Massachusetts stonemason Sonam Lama, who braved possible incarceration to return to his Chinese-occupied homeland of Tibet. As detailed in the film's opening passage, Lama had fled with two young companions twelve years before; after establishing his American citizenship, Sonam returned to visit his surviving family (culminating in a reunion with his older sister Karma, who raised him), bringing with him the blessings of His Holiness the Dalai Lama. In the end, Sonam led his fourteen-year-old niece Yangchen and eight-year-old cousin Lhamo out of Tibet for a new life in India.

That, of course, was not the end of the story. Sonam is still living and working in Greenfield, and remains a passionate advocate and activist for the cause of his homeland. He employs many Tibetan exiles in his own business, and continues to work for the collective good of his family and people.

"Yangchen is here," Lisa tells us, *"in the U.S.. She came three or four years ago. It took a long time to get her here. Sonam is her uncle, and he tried to get her to come for many years, but it was just really hard. Finally, he was able to sponsor her, through talking to* [Massachusetts Senators] *Ted Kennedy and John Kerry and doing whatever he could. It wasn't easy at all."*

Subsequently, Yangchen was almost deported back to Tibet. *"She had four years on an education visa,"* Lisa continues. *"They realized they had to to something, because when her time came up, she would go back – and where would she go? Would she go to India? Would she go to Tibet? If she went to Tibet, what would happen to her? They got an immigration lawyer and applied for political asylum."* Alan continues, *"Yangchen came to a private school here in New England, where she's now the equivalent of eleventh grader in high school, although she's twenty."*

Home to Tibet played a primary role in Yangchen's successful bid for American citizenship. *"The main reason she was granted asylum was because the film had depicted her family, her background, and everything,"* Alan says. *"If the Chinese saw it, they would say, 'This is clearly anti-Chinese, let's put you in jail immediately.' So she couldn't go back because of the film. She got asylum. That was an unexpected benefit on this side."*

"On the same hand, if this film were shown in Tibet, and the Chinese saw it, they would go immediately and find Karma and her family and put them into hard labor," Alan adds. Fortunately, *Home to Tibet* remains 'beneath the radar': it has not stirred enough international notoriety to endanger Sonam's relatives, though it continues to be shown around the world. *"The Chinese have bigger fish to fry,"* Lisa notes, citing the controversy recently aroused by the documentary *Windhorse* (1999), *"but that's always smoldering under the surface; it's being shown in Basil, Switzerland right now, at an exhibition of Tibetan art the Dalai Lama is opening."*

And what of eight-year-old Lhamo? *"Lhamo went to a private school in India,"* Alan says, *"to learn how to read and write English and Tibetan. She's still there, and wants to come here. We're still trying to figure out a way to get her to come live in the area."* Lisa adds, *"She needs a sponsor. Her parents want her – their only child – to come. America is still the land of fortune, it's still the promised land... the opportunities here are incredible."*

While living in India, Tibetan exile Geshe-La provided a safe haven for Sonam and many other Tibetan refugees; he is another key figure in *Home to Tibet* who has since established a new life for himself stateside. Geshe-La's reason for moving to the U.S. is grounded in one of the more arcane aspects of Tibetan politics. *"He is in the United States because of a 'protector' called Dorje Shugden that certain Tibetans worship, and other do not,"* Lisa explains. *"The Dalai Lama at some point declared that Dorje Shugden was 'taboo,' and there was a lot of in-fighting among the Tibetans. Geshe-La was a Dorje Shugden worshiper, so his house was firebombed, people were killed. So, Geshe-La got political asylum, too, and is living in Minnesota with his whole family, where he is teaching."*

"That element of Tibetan strife is unfortunate, because it has really divided people, though some of it has settled down," Lisa notes. *"People are people,"* Alan adds, *"no matter where you go, even peace-loving people will do harm to each other if they feel they have to."*

Alan is quick to clarify that such violence is hardly typical of the Tibetan situation. *"There's a scene in the film where the people are walking on the street, and to me that really sums up and characterizes it,"* director Alan Dater says. *"The Tibetan people are really depressed, really down-trodden, second-class citizens in their own country. I remember Yangchen saying that she looked up to the Chinese people because they were the way to be, that was what she was brought up to see; they were 'better.' You really saw a change in Yangchen when she came here; she was just hungry for learning and educational experiences, she just worked so hard. She's trying really hard to get a good education so she can go back and help her people – maybe not in Tibet, but somewhere, to contribute to their greater good."*

"The whole thing about leaving..." Lisa says, *"the Dalai Lama is really mixed about that. Should people leave? The country is being depleted if people keep leaving."* And yet, by carving out their own niches in the world, embracing educational opportunities, and telling their own stories, Sonam, Yangchen, Lhamo, and Geshe-La and other Tibetans who have sought asylum and new lives outside Tibet have done more for their homeland than they could have ever done in their villages.

"I think every Tibetan here without exception is sending money home every time they can," Lisa adds. *"They're all doing everything they can for Tibet. There is this incredible pipeline of support and hope that feeds that place."*

Sonam has assumed legendary stature among his people, feeding that hope in many ways. *"Yes, I think that's a really appropriate word: he is legendary in his homeland,"* Lisa says, *"and in a lot of Tibetan eyes here, too. He's just been really generous."*

That generosity of spirit also fuels Lisa and Alan's household and work. It is the heart and soul of *Home to Tibet*.

June 2:

SHADOW OF THE VAMPIRE: As a lifelong horror film aficionado, I am both amused and disgusted by the occasional spectacle of mainstream critics tripping over themselves to heap praise on genre curios. They inevitably malign the truly potent, dangerous, and influential horror films (*Psycho*, 1960, *Night of the Living Dead*, 1968, *The Texas Chainsaw Massacre*, 1974, *Eraserhead*, 1977, etc.), only to make up for missing the boat by heaping undue praise on tamer ferry excursions (*Jaws*,

1975, *Halloween*, 1978, *Alien*, 1979, *Scream*, 1996, *The Blair Witch Project*, 1999, etc.).

Such is the case with E. Elias Merhige's *Shadow of the Vampire* (2000), an interesting failure that has won accolades from critics despite the fact that it neither works as a horror film, a black comedy, a drama, or a meditation on cinema. Mind you, it isn't a terrible film, and there is some fun to be had – thanks primarily to Willem Dafoe – but the rave reviews seem to be about another film altogether.

Ironically, critics (with a few notable exceptions) missed director E. Elias Merhige's debut feature, *Begotten* (1991), a genuinely nightmarish creation that stands among the most terrifying expressionistic films ever made. Most still haven't the means to assess Merhige's unnerving, almost alchemical 'trance' film, which malingered over its dreamlike agonies and transmutations via tactile and increasingly obscured imagery (approach with caution: casual viewers will loathe *Begotten* if they get beyond the first five minutes). It was brave of actor-turned-producer Nicholas Cage to entrust a narrative studio film like *Shadow of the Vampire* to Merhige, a decision comparable to comedian-turned-producer Mel Brooks' choice of David Lynch to direct the Victorian romance of *The Elephant Man* (1980) on the strength of Lynch's surreal 'midnight movie' *Eraserhead*. Merhige rose to the challenge, and this, his first mainstream effort, is certainly an ambitious and compelling work. I'm pleased that the relative success of *Shadow* means Merhige will be hopefully be employed for years to come; no working commercial filmmaker could build a career on a primal, impenetrable non-narrative feature like *Begotten*.[13]

I only wish *Shadow of the Vampire* were a better film. Though the studio may have felt it had superficial similarities to Bill Condon's excellent *Gods and Monsters* (1998), *Shadow* succumbs to its own shallow premise long before it reaches its climax. Screenwriter Steven Katz proffers that the star of F. W. Murnau's classic vampire film *Nosferatu: A Symphony of Terror* (*Nosferatu, Eine Symphonie des Grauens*, 1922) was, in fact, a vampire. An amusing notion, that, but don't take the film at face value: Katz never lets facts get in the way of his rather clumsy fabrications. The script cheats time and time again in its portrait of *Nosferatu* itself; Merhige intercuts actual footage from *Nosferatu* with maladroit 'recreations' of key images, at which it more often than not fails miserably. The depiction of silent filmmaking technology and techniques is a sham, and the film is littered with anachronistic errors. One choice bit of dialogue has Murnau being compared – in 1921 – to film pioneers D.W. Griffith and Russian director Sergei Eisenstein, two years before Eisenstein's first short film (*Dnevnik Glumova*, 1923) and a full *four years* before Eisenstein made his first feature film *Strike* (*Stachka*, 1925) and his masterpiece *Battleship Potemkin* (*Bronenosets Potyomkin*, 1925). In short, there's no way anyone in Germany knew who Eisenstein was in 1921, folks. I reckon Katz skipped or failed Film Studies 101 before selling the script; Heaven forbid someone should do any real research.

---

[13] Merhige has since directed the compelling *Suspect Zero* (2004) and the exquisite experimental short *Din of Celestial Birds* (2006), available at http://www.dinofcelestialbirds.com

The central conceit of *Shadow* is spelled out in an early line of dialogue, as the lead actress (Catherine McCormack) of *Nosferatu* complains about the camera, saying, *"A theatrical audience gives me life, while this* thing *merely takes it from me."* Thus, cinema is itself a vampire, a parasitic medium that feeds on the essence of those who participate. To that end, *Shadow of the Vampire* depicts the remarkable German director Friedrich Wilhelm Murnau (overplayed by John Malkovich) as a petty tyrant, willing to sacrifice cast and crew to the insatiable appetites of the very genuine bloodsucker (Willem Dafoe) to complete his illegal pastiche of Bram Stoker's *Dracula* while rambling on about art and science. Thus, Murnau was the first 'snuff film' maker.

Whether taken as an unfair caricature or outright character assassination, the end result is an arch, pretentious film that only comes to life when Dafoe graces the screen as the inhuman Max Schrek. Though Dafoe is as shamelessly hammy as Malkovich, he is far, far more entertaining. He relishes every line as if he were sucking an old bandaid for nourishment, moving with the measured reserve of a being breaking the grip of rigor mortis with every step, nervously clacking his elongated fingernails together when he frets, and fidgeting like a caged rat when his cravings overwhelm him.

The film's finest setpiece arrives when Schrek stumbles into a drunken after-hours conversation between *Nosferatu* producer and art director Albin Grau (Udo Keir, in the film's slyest casting coup: he played *Andy Warhol's Dracula* in 1974) and writer Henrik Galeen (Aden Gillett).[14] Drunk and confused, still believing Schrek to be an actor lost in his role rather than a real creature of the night, the revelers offer Schrek their bottle of Schnapps. They have no idea what to make of it when he answers their questions about Stoker's novel with sad candor, empathizing completely with the infamous Count's sorry lot, and are unexpectedly gob smacked when Schrek plucks a bat out of the air and noisily slurps it down. The sequence captures the all-too-familiar tenor of late-night party non-conversations before deftly pitching into an unexpected revelation of Schrek's true nature that is both hilarious and frightening. For one marvelous moment, *Shadow of the Vampire* plucks the precise chord it has fumbled around, a note it fails to sustain or approach ever again.

To address the obvious: No, Max Schrek was *not* a vampire; he was indeed a member of the famous Max Reinhardt theatrical troupe and a character actor who appeared in over 30 German films between 1920 and 1936, including *The Street* (*Die Strasse*, 1923) and *The Tunnel* (*Der Tunnel*, 1933). Nor was Murnau a despotic 'snuff film' maker; he was one of the premiere filmmakers of his era, a visual artist without peer in his time. Devote the evening *Shadow of the Vampire* sucks dry to just *one* of Murnau's masterpieces – *The Last Laugh* (1924) or his epic adaptation of *Faust* (1926) – and you will see what magic Murnau and the German cinema was capable of. Better yet, see Murnau's *Nosferatu* (the Kino restoration is the best) instead of, or before, *Shadow of the Vampire*.

---

[14] Interesting regional historical note: Galeen lived out his final years in my home state of Vermont, dying in Randolph, VT on July 30, 1949.

There's a reason filmmakers are still plundering *Nosferatu* eighty years hence: it remains one of the best horror films ever made. Even with his hands tied behind his back – by a low budget, poor shooting conditions, and a wretched lead performance by the film's nominal 'hero' – Murnau created a masterpiece. This is more than those responsible for *Shadow of the Vampire* can claim. Filmmaker E. Elias Merhige may yet merit comparison to Murnau: as an expressionist nightmare, *Begotten* is a worthy successor to *Nosferatu*, whereas *Shadow of the Vampire* is a hollow pastiche. Don't forget that Werner Herzog stumbled with his unnecessary (but still fascinating) 1979 remake of *Nosferatu*; Merhige is, at least, in good company.

As usual, the DVD presentation is superior. Throughout the special features, the filmmakers discuss their struggle with the film's title, fearful that their creation would be dismissed as *"just another vampire movie."* In the end, though, it *is* just another vampire movie – less than that, it's a vampire *art* movie, a bloodless taxidermy specimen. However noble their intentions (if character assassination, however unintended, can be considered honorable) and impeccable their artistic credentials, the makers of *Shadow of the Vampire* do not deserve the praise showered upon them by those who remain blind to, and fearful of, the real power of the horror film. I'll forever prefer mine straight, no chaser. *(Rated 'R' for language, adult and sexual content, alcohol and drug use, and violence.)*

SHORT CUTS (Recent & Recommended):

Who needs vampires? Though *Shadow of the Vampire* is dominating the chiller video rentals this month, those of you in search of real shudders should check out these 'sleepers':

FEVER: Alex Winter is best known for his co-starring lead (alongside buddy Keanu Reeves) in *Bill and Ted's Excellent Adventure* (1989); his filmmaking accomplishments are less renowned, though deserving of greater attention. As a film student, Winter teamed with classmate Tom Stern to make riotous short films like *Squeal of Death* (1983). Winter and Stern's studio feature directorial debut *Freaked* (1993) remains one of funniest black comedies of its decade, though parent studio 20th Century Fox 'freaked' and buried it. That financial debacle tabled Winter's directing career until now. His most recent solo effort *Fever* (2000) reaffirms Winter's directorial skills in a decidedly darker vein, as lonely art instructor and painter Henry Thomas (*E.T., All the Pretty Horses*) mentally unravels in his sordid New York City apartment after his landlord is brutally murdered. No one has ever topped Roman Polanski's subjective portraits of isolation and madness in *Repulsion* (1965) and *The Tenant* (1976), but Winters brings his own distinctive (if uncharacteristically understated) touch to the genre. *Fever* got to me, and David O'Hara (*Braveheart*) is particularly chilling as the enigmatic tenant upstairs who may, or may not, be real. *(Rated 'R' for brief but graphic violence, nudity, and strong language.)*

SEE THE SEA: This new video release of two short films by French writer/director François Ozon features lovely oceanside locales and explores, uh, alternative lifestyles. The collection opens with the light *The Summer Dress* (*Une Robe d'Eté*, 1997), in which a gay young man (Frédéric Mangenot) discovers the joys of bisexuality and the titular garment, setting a deceptively amiable tone for its disturbing companion *See the Sea* (*Regarde la Mer*, 1997). A young mother (Sasha Hails) essentially stranded in her beachside home by the absence of her husband welcomes an enigmatic nomad (Marina De Van) to camp on her lawn. The wanderer both covets and loathes the bond between mother and child, with truly dire results. The film creeps up and under the skin; it's as chilling and insidious a meditation on genuine human evil as George Sluizer's original *The Vanishing* (*Spoorloos*, 1988). Brrrrrr: brave souls shouldn't miss it, but all others, beware. *(Unrated; though there is no onscreen violence, this is not for the squeamish or viewers under 18 years of age; both films feature nudity, adult and sexual activity, and the latter also features scatological content.)*

June 14:

CROUCHING TIGER, HIDDEN DRAGON: Though mainstream American audiences have always considered superheroes part and parcel of comicbooks (and comicbook adaptations to film, such as *Batman* and *The X-Men*), the superhero archetype is an ancient one that is common to many cultures. The Greeks and Romans had their Gods, heroes, and monsters; the Native Americans their warriors, seers, shamans, and elemental beings; and the Chinese had their 'wuxia,' or 'roaming hero,' tales. In these, nomadic heroes (male and female) were endowed with superhuman abilities, brilliant masters and fighters who adhered to rigid codes of honor to their deaths. Such is the world of *Crouching Tiger, Hidden Dragon* (*Wo Hu Cang Long*, 2000), where the escalating confrontations between a quartet of seemingly superhuman warriors sends them soaring over battlefields, ledges, rooftops, and into the trees in intoxicating displays of grace, power, and uncanny skill. These setpieces have the breathtaking allure of half-remembered dreams, where we have all, at one time or another, soared into and over the trees and plunged into the unknown.

Such spectacle was no doubt central to the breakthrough success of *Crouching Tiger, Hidden Dragon* in America, where this foreign-language, subtitled-in-English epic kicked aside all previous records to score an unprecedented $100 million at the boxoffice (those of you who resisted its charms *because* it was subtitled, take heart: there is an English-dubbed version on video and, accompanying the subtitled original, on DVD). The remarkable synthesis of period action, adventure, romance, costumes, locations, performances, and music (the film is beautifully scored by Tan Dun) proved irresistible, and all its virtues make the leap to home video intact – though, as always, the DVD is particularly recommended for the crystalline clarity of image, audio, and the delicious extras (including the commentary track from director Ang Lee, documentaries on Michelle Yeoh and the making of the film, and more).

The nighttime theft of the legendary Green Destiny sword is the catalyst for all that ensues. The elite Wudan warrior who wielded the sword, Li Mu Bai (Chow Yun Fat of John Woo's *The Killer/Dip Huet Seung Hung*, 1989, *Hard-Boiled/Lat Sau San Taam*, 1992, and recent American efforts like *The Replacement Killer*, 1998, *The Corruptor* and *Anna and the King*, both 1999[15]), joins forces with the lovely Yu Shu Lien (Michelle Yeoh of

---

[15] See *Blur, Vol. 1*, pp. 46-47, and *Blur, Vol. 2*, pp. 112-114.

Supercop/Ging Chaat Goo Si 3: Chiu Kap Ging Chaat, 1992, *The Heroic Trio/Dung Fong Saam Hap*, 1993, and the James Bond film *Tomorrow Never Dies*, 1997) to regain the sword. Though masters of the martial arts, neither Li nor Yu can express their love for one another, bound by their duty, their moral code, and a shared past that keeps them apart. Yu suspects the thief to be a Governor's daughter, Jen Yu (Zhang Zi Ya), who is in the thrall of Li's mortal enemy Jade Fox (Cheng Pei Pei). Complicating the entangled pasts, paths, and intrigue is Jen Yu's unrequited love for a bandit chieftain (Chang Chen) – and at the heart of it all is the almost mystical power of the Green Destiny, around which all their fates revolve.

This ravishing, opulent period martial arts epic from director Ang Lee (returning to his home country after helming English and American gems like *Sense and Sensibility*, 1995, *The Ice Storm*, 1997, and *Ride With the Devil*, 1999[16]) deservedly captivated international audiences – except, curiously enough, Ang Lee's native country, where the film was reportedly laughed at by Mandarin audiences bemused by the stars' odd accents and arch dialogue delivery. This brings to mind my own love for spaghetti westerns (hang with me, now, I do have a point to make), where the dubbed English versions of classics like Sergio Leone's *For A Few Dollars More/Per Qualche Dollaro in Più* (1965) and *The Good, The Bad, and The Ugly/ Il Buone, Il Brutto, Il Cattivo* (1966) carried their own bizarre charm. For me, the fact that the dialogue sounded like it had been post-synched (it had; during filming, the performers each spoke their native tongues – English, Italian, German, Spanish – and

---

[16] See *Blur, Vol. 2*, pp. 187-188.

final dubbing for each respective market cleaned up the soundtrack) only added to the dream-like hyper-reality of Leone's westerns. I later read that for Leone, the vagaries of post-synched sound (i.e., dialogue never matching lip movement, the oddly detached quality of the audio and sound effects) was essential to a 'true western,' as every American western he had ever seen growing up had been dubbed into Italian!

Along with Sam Peckinpah (director of *Ride the High Country*, 1962, and *The Wild Bunch*, 1969), Leone became the primary visionary of the autumn decade of the western. Leone potently summarized the essence of the entire genre in his epic *Once Upon a Time in the West/C'era Una Volta il West* (1968); thereafter, one measured the genre by the films made before, and those made after, Leone's masterpiece. *Once Upon a Time in the West* captured all that made the myth of the west resonate, reassessing that myth with the jaundiced eye of a 1960s artist looking back at the corruption and capitalism that had edged the American belief in Manifest Destiny into the harsh realities of the Industrial Era. It was the end of an era, Leone knew, and he marked its passing (and that of *"an ancient race,"* to quote a line of dialogue from the film) with his finest creation.

That is Ang Lee's accomplishment, too, with *Crouching Tiger, Hidden Dragon*. Hereafter, all films of its kind will be measured by whether they were made before or after *Crouching Tiger*. Lee has embodied, into a single film, the essence of the great and near-great Asian martial arts and 'swordplay' films, historical romances, Chinese theater, and the rich folk legends that inspired them. Like Leone, he not only captures their mythic power, but reinterprets and rekindles that primal allure anew with passion, energy, humor, and heartfelt gravity. *Crouching Tiger, Hidden Dragon* ranks high among the best films of this or any year, and is not to be missed. *(Rated 'PG-13' for violence, adult and sexual content.)*

SHORT CUTS (Recent & Recommended):

***ONCE UPON A TIME IN CHINA I* and *II (Wong Fei Hung* and *Wong Fei Hung II: Naam Yi Dong Ji Keung*):** If you want to experience the cream of the crop of the martial arts epics that inspired *Crouching Tiger, Hidden Dragon*, look no further than this pair of Jet Li historical actioners (made in 1991 and '92). The premiere alchemist of the Hong Kong cinema transformation of the 1980s and '90s was protean producer / director Tsui Hark (pronounced 'Choy Hock'), and these were two of his breakthrough martial arts epics. The incredible boxoffice success of the first installment throughout Asia made Jet Li (real name: Li Lian Jie) a superstar in his home country, prompting the torrent of Jet Li features currently claiming prime space on video new release walls.

Li stars as the revered Chinese hero Wong Fei-hong, a turn-of-the-century master of the martial arts and a renowned herbalist and physician who almost single-handedly mobilized China and Hong Kong against encroaching Western powers and the complicity of corrupt local authorities. This historical tug-of-war is vividly rendered with high romance, chivalry, villainy, and eye-popping battle sequences. Li starred in the first three of the series, with Hark directing all but one (the fourth installment). Though the high spirits began to wane in the third (coming soon to home video), *Once Upon a*

Time in China I and *II* are magnificent films, and highly recommended.

This past Monday night, Brattleboro's own Center for Digital Art had a public showing of the final video projects of this year's Digital Editing class. Running between ten to fifteen minutes each, this eclectic selection made for a lively evening's entertainment.

There were six short films shown: Alicia Swartz's ***Morbid Earth***, in which a simulcrum of the Earth is tortured, voodoo-like, with pins, flame, wax, etc., crosscut with the human toll of this magic (rape, murder, suicide, etc.), until the final apocalyptic devastation; Jesse-Cross Nickerson's ***The Pursuit***, a compellingly fragmented account of a teenager eluding (with the help of an enigmatic, almost spectral woman) two hunters intent on killing him; Pat Matteau's ***The Decline***, chronicling the slide of a teenage boy (Ethan Kerr) from loneliness and boredom into alcoholism and violence; Ian Reynolds' ***Ski Video***, a lively montage of Ian and his friends skiing (and carrying on to and from the slopes) set to an invigorating musical score – Warren Miller, look out!; Ashley J. Randall's ***On Christmas Eve***, a heartful, truly devotional portrait of her grandmother Joyce W. Pelos, a librarian in Jamaica, VT who composed the titular Christmas song and savors a recent local high school performance of her creation, while, with the help of her friend and companion Warren Patrick, she seeks to interest music publishers and record companies in her work; and Andrew Hayes' taut, suspenseful ***Staying Alive***, an ambitious mini-thriller in which a hitman (Sean Ahern) spurns his employer and risks life and limb to save a young woman slated for a hit.

This is the second class showcase I've had the pleasure of attending, and the diversity of subject, tenor, and tone of the work is remarkable. The sometimes mature content level is indicative of the class' strengths and vitality, not a liability or cause for undue controversy; healthy expression, not repression, is the keyword here. The students' ambitions are occasionally frustrated by their reach (determined, in part, by their age, the available means, and the tight time frames they are all working within), but this was a remarkably accomplished batch of short films, on a par with or better than the work I saw from many Vermont colleges this year. Kudos to all the filmmakers, to instructors Michel and Linda Moyse, to the Career Center, and to BUHS[17]! This is a class well worth the level of community support it continues to receive – and mark my words, in the not-too-distant future, you'll be enjoying the pro efforts of one or more of these graduates in a theater or video store near you.[18]

June 17:

CAST AWAY: For major studios and most contemporary American audiences, the rematch of star Tom Hanks and director Robert Zemeckis (*Back to the Future*, 1985, *Who Framed Roger Rabbit?*, 1988, *Contact*, 1997, etc.)

---

[17] Brattleboro Union High School in Brattleboro, VT.

[18] We've already seen at least two CDA graduates land professional work on commercially available DVDs: David Gutt's Boston-based Subversion Media video work includes *The Pixies: Sell Out 2004 Reunion Tour* (2005); visit Subversion Media's website at http://www.subversionmedia.com and their MySpace page at http://www.myspace.com/mediasubversion Andrew Hayes worked (ass't camera, second unit) on Jay Craven's feature *Disappearances* (2006).

is a match made in Heaven – well, Hollywood heaven, in any case. Studio logic dictates that the team behind *Forrest Gump* (1994) can do no wrong, and there was a certain reckless bravery in Hanks and Zemeckis jumping into *Cast Away* (2000) with such relative abandon (relative because, well, I don't think either of them could truly give themselves over to a reckless muse).

In the opening, we see FedEx employee extraordinaire Chuck Noland (Hanks) training workers 'round the world, wrestling with cultural aversions to anything resembling 'timely delivery,' before rushing back stateside just long enough to establish his work-strained relationship with his sweetie Kelly (Helen Hunt) before he's off on a plane again for (literally) parts unknown. The plane plunges into the drink in yet another harrowing plane crash (as if those in *Alive, Fearless* – both 1993 – and *Final Destination*, 2000, didn't set the bar high enough), setting the story proper into action – or, in stark contrast to the majority of Zemeckis' hyperactive movies, inaction.

Stranded alone on a remote isle, Chuckie-baby struggles through the *Robinson Crusoe* schtick, sans Friday (unless you count his soccer-ball pseudo-pal 'Wilson' as a surrogate Friday). Zemeckis and Hanks milk the situation for all the desperation, angst, and skewed humor they can muster in a mainstream Hollywood vehicle. The film chronicles the first few weeks with loving detail, capturing Chuck's ingenious use of his salvaged FedEx shipments, the island's meager resources, and the first evidence of the fellow's slipping sanity, until an impromptu but necessary bit of dental surgery sends the camera wheeling away from Chuck's agony and the screenplay lurching ahead years (I kid you not) – *four years*.

Now, this is the point in the filming when director and star parted ways long enough for Hanks to shed pounds and grow a scraggly salt-and-pepper beard while Zemeckis squeezed another entire film (the shrill, shabby filmed-in-Vermont thriller *What Lies Beneath* with Harrison Ford and Michelle Pfeiffer[19]) out like – well, I won't go there; suffice to mention, that might be when Zemeckis conceived the importance of a plastic portapotty to the conclusion of *Cast Away*.

Anyhoot, *four years* later, the film rejoins the gaunt, cross-wired Chuck for the final act of his island seclusion, setting up an extended epilogue that plugs back into the opening act and ties up the loose ends. For me, the film never recovered from shying away from the real survival tale in its rush to rejoin Chuck after the worst had passed. It's a classic Republican move, really – *"let's skip the messy/boring survival bits and just cut to the chase!"* – and as such, true to the pervasive Bush-era redux denial of the underbellies of life.

Hanks gives the film his all, as always, remaining utterly likable throughout even as he indulges in the sort of method madness that served Robert DeNiro well in *Raging Bull* (1980) and Nick Nolte in *Affliction* (1997, which held the previous record for *"most-grueling-Hollywood-do-it-yourself-dentistry"*),[20] and I can't fault any aspect of his performance, which indeed holds our attention through the long stretches of dialogue-free screentime. But the screenplay's episodic structure,

---

[19] See *Blur, Vol. 3*, pp. 118-119.

[20] Add Christian Bale to the 'method madness' legends for starving himself – from 180 pounds to an excrutiating 120 pounds – to play the lead in Brad Anderson and Scott Kosar's unnerving *El Maquinista/ The Machinist* (2004).

clumsily framing the core narrative with an ephemeral FedEx fillip only to flinch away from it's real heart – the duration of Chuck's isolation – only emphasizes the shallowness of the entire enterprise. It would have taken a tougher American director like the late Robert Aldrich (who fashioned a grueling, gritty survivalist tale out of *The Flight of the Phoenix* back in 1965) or a visionary like Nicolas Roeg (directing *Walkabout*, 1971, in his prime and *Castaway*, 1986, later) to bring genuine life to this rather flimsy potboiler.

I don't mean to badmouth Zemeckis – I quite like some of his films – but *Cast Away* never approaches the level of drama it aspires (or pretends) to. To communicate hunger, isolation, and desperation with conviction, a filmmaker must have tasted the life experience necessary to bring meat to the bones of *Cast Away*'s skeletal form. Given the final result, I suspect Zemeckis hasn't really been hungry a single day of his life, particularly over the last twenty years of Hollywood success he has earned and savored. In fact, Zemeckis' earlier rough-and-tumble black comedy *Used Cars* (1980) communicated a far more convincing air of cut-throat desperation and hunger; but at that time, Zemeckis (with only one other film under his belt) was hungry and desperate himself. Of course, Zemeckis-circa-2000 shied away from the reality of Chuck's situation, though one wonders how Hanks would have risen to the challenge had his director had the fortitude to see it through. *(Rated "PG" for language, nasty self-surgical techniques, and adult situations and content.)*

O BROTHER, WHERE ART THOU?: You can keep Zemeckis: I'll take the Coen Brothers (Joel and Ethan) any day of the week, and their latest confection is a giddy delight, though many urban critics seemed oblivious to its charms. The hell with 'em: take the ride, and have yourself a ball. Relevant to my above rant, *O Brother, Where Art Thou?* lifts its title and flavor from Preston Sturges' sardonic classic *Sullivan's Travels* (1941), a gutsy attack on Depression-era Hollywood's 'social cinema' in which a top-drawer director (Joel McCrea) sick of making comedies decides to research his planned 'serious' film by hitting the road as a hobo to taste hardship, hunger, and poverty. The Coen Brothers borrow their title from that McCrea's character concocts for his wanna-be significant opus, and cop the mix of quick wit, satire, and edgy dark humor that Sturges sustained so well in his masterpiece.

You don't have to be familiar with Homer's *Odússeia/The Odyssey* to enjoy the Coens' inventive cross-country romp across the Depression-era South, but it adds immeasurably to the pleasures in store for you. The Coens' windblown wanderer is Ulysses Everett McGill (George Clooney), who flees a chain gang chained at the ankle to good-natured simpleton Delmar (Tim Blake Nelson) and haywire, quick-tempered Pete (John Turturro). McGill has promised his partners an even split of $1.2 million in buried booty, but he's really out to recover his estranged wife Penny (Holly Hunter) and his brood before she ties the knot with a slick political campaign manager. The gubernatorial campaign weaves in and out of the rambling misadventures of Everett, Delmar, and Pete, as they snack on gophers-on-a-stick, are reborn in a river baptism ceremony, and cross paths with a trio of lullaby-crooning sirens along a river (who, Circe-like, seem to change Pete into a frog), a manic-depressive pirate (Michael Badalucco as 'Baby Face' Nelson), and a ravenous cyclopean con-artist

(John Goodman in another larger-than-life role for the Coens, as in their *Raising Arizona*, 1987, and *Barton Fink*, 1991).

On their heels bay the hounds of vindictive, goggled lawman Sheriff Cooley (Daniel Von Bargen); ahead lies the promised land of the stolen fortune; and above malingers their unlikely, dour, overweight 'guardian angel,' incumbent governor Pappy O'Daniel (Charles Durning), whose political fortunes prove to be linked with the misfit trio's just rewards. En route, Everett, Delmar, and Pete hook up with nomadic blues man Tommy (Chris Thomas King) just after his meeting at the crossroads with the devil, and end up recording a tune as 'The Soggy Bottom Boys,' which also plays a part in their potential redemption.

I could go on and on, but I won't. This is a film best discovered on your own; I envy you the first-time viewing. I've been back several times since, and I suspect you will, too. The musical score is a charmer (pick up the CD), the players in perfect tune with the Coens' offbeat rhythms, Roger Deakins' dust-bowl-tinged cinematography is intoxicating, and the film is magnificent. This one gets my highest recommendation, and remains my favorite film of the year to date. *(Rated "PG-13" for violence, language, and adult situations.)*

SHORT CUTS (Recent & Recommended):

THE BALLAD OF RAMBLIN' JACK: If you love the music in *O Brother*, you owe it to yourself to spend an evening with Aiyana Elliott's lively, moving documentary about her father, the beloved folk singer Ramblin' Jack Elliott. Born to a Brooklyn Jewish family, Elliott hit the road early in life to join the rodeo. Trusting to the four winds like a homeless Odysseus without a destination, Elliott eventually hooked up with Woody Guthrie and began his own life as a wandering minstrel, picking and singing his way into folk legend.

Aiyana crafts a loving portrait of her wayward father, creating an engaging tapestry out of the fabric of salvaged home movies, interviews with Elliott, Pete Seeger, Arlo and Nora Guthrie, and both of Jack's wives, among others, and extensive footage of Elliott on the road and in concert around the world. This is a marvelous, stirring piece, basking in the glow of Elliott's warmth and expansive talents, deserving of (and sure to reward) your attention. Don't miss it. *(Rated "PG-13" for language, adult content.)*

June 28:

STATE AND MAIN: The fanciful town of Waterford, Vermont is shaken by the intrusion of Hollywood filmmakers in writer-director David Mamet's latest opus *State and Main* (2000), new to video this month and of particular local interest for what it isn't as much as what it is.

State and Main is about a film crew turning small-town Vermont upside-down.

But it *isn't* made in Vermont.

In the deft opening moments, a film crew (on the run from scandal at their prior New Hampshire location) scouts Waterford as the ideal new local for their production of *The Old Mill*. *"This is what my people died for – the right to make a movie in this town,"* declares director Walt Price (played by the extraordinary William H. Macy, part-time VT resident, Goddard College graduate and vet of *Fargo*, 1996, and Mamet films *The Water Engine*,

1992, and *Oleanna*, 1994, among others). In mere hours, they've claimed the local hotel as their base, and Mamet establishes the individual tics and schtick of his rogue's gallery. Director Price bulldozes all obstacles aside with measured finesse or callousness, as required; timid screenwriter Joseph Turner White (Philip Seymour Hoffman) struggles with his first film assignment, confounded by the loss of his beloved typewriter and need to replace the titular 'Old Mill' with some other metaphoric device; star Bob Berrenger (Alec Baldwin) basks in celebrity and indulges his appetite for fourteen-year-old girls; actress Claire Wellesley (Sarah Jessica Parker) – aka 'The Broad' – agonizes over a contractually-required nude scene; cinematographer Uberto Pazzi-Storza (Vincent Guastaferro) is confounded by an opening shot that simply won't work with the historic Waterford fire station stained-glass window in the way; producer Marty Rossen (David Paymer) manages damage control with caustic intensity.

Ah, but *The Old Mill* brings fresh opportunities to Waterford's bucolic eden. As the intrusive production reaches critical mass, the locals assert their own agendas. Community theater director Ann (Rebecca Pidgeon, Mamet's wife) has her upcoming play scuttled by film auditions, but her growing attraction to playwright White blossoms at the expense of her bond with fiancee Doug Mackenzie (Clark Gregg). Mackenzie soothes his aching heart by fanning the flames of conflict between the town and the Hollywood invaders, fueling his own political aspirations, while Mayor Bailey (Charles Durning) curries favor with the film folk to slake the societal elitism of his wife Maude (Charlotte Potok) with an all-important dinner with the cast, director, and producer. Meanwhile, the seeds of destruction for one and all are sown by teenage Carla (Julia Stiles), who knowingly targets Bob Berrenger's scandalous sexual proclivities.

Thus, Mamet sets the stage for an almost classical screwball comedy. But Mamet's distinctive style (with precision-delivery of his trademark clipped dialogue servicing narratives played with the calculated finesse of a chess match) is fundamentally at odds with the antic necessities of the genre, transmuting his script's ore into something other than gold. It is, in its intellectual way, as contrived as Peter Bogdonavich's *What's Up, Doc?* (1972), a failed pastiche of 1940s screwball comedies; Mamet's film, at least, is true to its own ideosyncratic muse. What, exactly, *State and Main* becomes depends entirely upon your own orientation to Mamet's dramatic (here, comedic) flourishes, which remain too arch and mannered for some viewers.

At its heart, the film indeed addresses its overt themes – corruption vs. innocence, the redemptive necessity of second chances – and in the enjoyable DVD commentary track, cast member David Paymer confirms the relative accuracy of its satiric portrait of filmmakers vs. community. Paymer notes that it is *"very common* [for filmmaking crews] *to live under that sense, like you're at war...* [that] *something terrible has either just happened, or is about to happen, or you're in dread that it's going to happen."* William Macy adds, *"Dave's been around a lot of movies on a lot of locations, so he knows what it does to a small town.... Every time you do a movie, with the exception of being on a studio, this is the story."*

As a fan of Mamet's work, I quite enjoyed *State and Main*. For a film that proclaims, via an early line delivered by director Price, *"It's not a lie – it's a gift for fiction,"* *State and Main* plays rather fast and loose with its lies, undercutting an otherwise-tight construction with a bit of cinematic flimflam – which I won't give away here – and one blatant cheat, which I will. Rewind (or quick scene access on the DVD) proves that the production white board notice that ultimately precipitates disaster (a crew member accidentally wipes off the note for the dinner date with the Mayor and his wife) is fudged late in the game to serve a needed twist of the blade in the penultimate act. Tut, tut, Mr. Mamet; it's not like you to bank on your audience's ignorance.

Such clumsy sleight-of-hand pales in the shadow of the key ruse of *State and Main*: it's a movie about filmmaking-in-Vermont that wasn't filmed in Vermont. Mamet, I'm told, used to teach at Marlboro College and live hereabouts; he and Macy were classmates at Goddard College. Among the props that lend *State and Main* a certain local flavor are copies of *The Brattleboro Reformer*, prominent in a sly sight gag involving Waterford locals Bunky (Morris Lamore) and Spud (Allen Soule; according to the DVD commentary track, both are Massachusetts poker cronies of Mamet's). When Bunky and Spud are first shown in the local diner, they're reading the *Reformer*, commenting on local issues; later in the film, once movie-fever has swept the community, the yokels are perusing their copies of *Variety* with rueful skepticism. Clever touch, that. But why wasn't *State and Main* made hereabouts?

As noted in the *Brattleboro Reformer*'s own article on the filming of *State and Main*,[21] Mamet ultimately selected Massachusetts location Manchester-by-the-Sea as a stand-in for Vermont. As noted in that article, *"stars*

---

[21] *"Vt. Film is Shot in Mass.," The Brattleboro Reformer*, Friday, October 1, 1999

and set-builders can more easily be transported from Boston than if the film were being made in, say, Montpelier." My own conversations with Loranne Turgeon, director of the Vermont Film Commission, confirm her frustration with the situation. Even as bigger-budget movies like *My, Myself and Irene* and *What Lies Beneath* were indeed being filmed in the Green Mountain State, budgetary restrictions kept *State and Main* out of state; the irony becomes especially thick when one learns that actor Clark Gregg ended up shuttling via helicopter between Mamet's Massachusetts location and Vermont, tending to the on-set rewrite needs of Gregg's script for *What Lies Beneath*. On the DVD commentary, William Macy offers a more personal reason for Mamet's decision: *"Dave has a rule that all the filmmaking he does has to be within a certain radius of his kitchen table."* Such is life. Don't let this sway you from the considerable pleasures of *State and Main*.

As already noted, your personal attraction or aversion to Mamet's stylistic flourishes should decide whether you visit *State and Main*. All in all, this is an amusing confection that rewards an evening's investment. Recommended! *(Rated 'R' for some partial nudity, adult and sexual situations, strong language.)*

SHORT CUTS (Recent & Recommended):

DUDE, WHERE'S MY CAR?: Dude, where's my movie?

BUTTERFLY: Don't miss next week's local fund-raising showing of this fine documentary (at – and to benefit – the Common Ground Restaurant, Elliott Street, on Tuesday, July 3rd). Filmmaker Doug Wolens lovingly chronicles the extraordinary dedication of young environmental activist Julia Butterfly Hill, who impulsively bonded with and climbed a thousand-year-old California redwood tree, ultimately living 180-feet-above-ground in its branches for over two years to protect the mighty 'Luna' (her affectionate name for the tree) from the chainsaw blades of loggers.

By doing so, Julia Hill attracted the patronage of Earth First environmental activists (who kept her supplied with food and necessities) and brought intensive media attention to the ongoing ravages of Pacific Lumber under new management. Wolens creates a persuasive portrait of Hill's private crusade, noting her own tangled relations with the activists, the media, her family, infuriated PL company representatives, bemused authorities, and the surrounding community of supporters and detractors (including loggers who lost their jobs due to Hill's successful stand-off). At the heart of it all lays Hill's almost mystical bond with Luna, which is also conveyed with uncluttered clarity.

Hill, the home-educated daughter of an Evangelical preacher, made her fateful climb while in her mid-20s, offering a potent new role model for a generation raised beneath the thumb of seemingly omnipotent corporate powers. Like our own Jim Jeffords,[22] Hill proves by her example that one person *can* make a difference in the new Millennium. Despite the often simplistic rhetoric of

---

[22] VT Senator James Jeffords left the Republican Party on May 24, 2001 to become an independent, changing the composition of the Senate from a Republican majority to 49 Republicans, 50 Democrats – a brief but major blow to President Bush's thin majority, until the Democrats lost the majority in 2003.

the various players in this real-life drama – from Hill's naive, but profoundly genuine, spirituality to Pacific Lumber proprietor Charles Hurwitz's proclamation *"he who has the gold, rules"* – director Wolens cunningly interweaves the various threads in this complex tapestry into a compelling film. Throughout, Wolens' mounts a potent analysis of the friction – and occasional harmony – between private versus collectivist activism, communal needs vs. corporate avarice, personal loss (including communities demolished by mud slides and a protester decapitated by a felled tree) vs. capitalist greed.

Butterfly was previously shown in the area as part of the Women's Film Festival, and makes its return visit to Brattleboro on behalf of the Common Ground;[23] special thanks to Richard Evers for bringing this to my attention and providing a screener. This is a vital work, and highly recommended.

July 5:

TRAFFIK: If you're tired of the summer fluff in the theaters this week, check out this 365-minute masterpiece, the original 1989 British TV miniseries recently adapted to the big screen as the multi-award-winning *Traffic* (2000). Much as I like Steven Soderbergh's feature, the original (written by Simon Moore and directed

---

[23] A personal note: I later joined the Board of Directors for the Common Ground, from 2005-2006, working to reopen the restaurant; the Common Ground, once world-famous as a successful worker-owned cooperative whole-and-organic foods restaurant, *did* reopen as a restaurant in 2006 – shortly after my formally resigning from the board – only to close less than a year later. At the time of this writing, its fate is still in limbo.

by Alastair Reid) is far, far superior, and not to be missed.

Unfolding in six episodes (on three video cassettes), *Traffik* weaves a complex dramatic tapestry out of three sets of characters – in Britain, Germany, and Pakistan – that creates a compelling, ultimately harrowing portrait of the international heroin trade. A British home office minister (Bill Paterson) wrestles with a pending drug treaty with Pakistan as his home life falls to pieces in the wake of his discovery of his daughter's (a very young Julia Ormond) heroin addiction; the wife (Lindsay Duncan) of a prominent Hamburg dealer (George Kukura) is forced into an escalating life of crime to salvage home and family in the wake of her husband's arrest and imprisonment; a displaced Pakistani farmer (Jamal Shah) is drawn into gainful employ with the area's drug kingpin (Talat Hussain) with disastrous consequences for his family.

The richer character detail and development suffered in the leap from the small to the big screen. The miniseries offers a far more expansive, truly adult perspective on the tragic 'war on drugs' and its ultimate futility. This is due, in part, to the longer running time; for instance, the plight of Lindsay Duncan's character is utterly believable, her transformation from blissful ignorance to tough, self-reliant ruthlessness persuasively nuanced. The hard education of Bill Paterson's diplomat to the ways of the world, and his stormy relations with his addict daughter, is also richer than Michael Douglas' corresponding role in the feature film adaptation, exploring depths the American feature seemed to shy away from.

The most crucial, and crippling, revision from miniseres to feature was the transplanting of locales (supplanting Pakistan with Mexico), and loss of the central Pakistan setting: Soderbergh's adaptation created a wholly new character (Benicio Del Toro's Mexican cop) in place of the uprooted opium farmer Fazal (Jamal Shah), whose profoundly moving story plunges the viewer into the black heart of the heroin trade.

By skirting the spidery source of all the corruption, collusion, addiction, denial, and betrayal at the center of its web, the feature film version of *Traffic* cut itself from the root of all evil exposed in *Traffik*. This brilliant Brit original succinctly summarizes the weaker *Traffic* with a single line in its fourth episode (wherein a Pakistan smuggler dismisses US intervention with the line, *"America's never a problem as long as it's fighting itself"*), while exploring deeper political, social, human, and dramatic turf every step of the way.[24] Highest recommendation! *(Unrated, but consider this the equivalent of a strong 'R' for its uncompromising adult content, including violence, nudity and sexual content, strong language, and vivid depiction of drug trade and abuse.)*

SHORT CUTS (Recent & Recommended):

DRACULA 2000: The masthead says *"Wes Craven Presents,"* as if the director of *The Last House on the Left* (1972), *The Hills Have Eyes* (1977), *A Nightmare on Elm Street* (1984), and *Scream* (1996), among others, had anything to do with this. Alas, Wes was busy elsewhere – which could be a good thing, depending on Craven's relative proximity to his muse of late. The di-

---

[24] In August 2008, the British *Traffik* remains incredibly relevant, given the US's botched war in Afghanistan; it's still essential viewing.

rector of this latest millennial vampire opus is actually Patrick Lussier, helming a so-so script that incorporates fillips from Marv Wolfman and Gene Colan's venerable 1970s Marvel Comic series *Tomb of Dracula* (from whence sprung *Blade*, 1998) to posit a contemporary Van Helsing generation (led by Christopher Plummer, delivering the only real performance on view) still keeping the classic Count down.

A team of high-tech thieves break into the Van Helsing high-security vault in London; instead of the expected booty, they accidentally unleash Dracula himself into the 21st century. Among the occasional amusements is Danny Masterson (who plays Hyde on *That 70s Show*) as the first victim; at one point, he's prying a hyperactive leech off his eyelid, stretching 'em both *waaaay* out. Hey, I'll take my summer kicks wherever I can find 'em. After chowing on Masterson, Drac is en route to New Orleans, targeting the next Van Helsing in line (Justine Waddell) with vampire-hunters Van Helsing and his ward (Jonny Lee Miller of *Trainspotting*, 1996) hot on his trail. It's all hooey, but Omar Epps, Jeri Ryan, and Jennifer Esposito add some fresh blood to the proceedings, which are sparked with some heavier-than-expected Judeo-Christian twists in the tail proffering a fresh context for Dracula's origins. If you're an undemanding horror fan looking for light scare fare for a hot summer night, this will do, just. *(Rated 'R' for violence, gore, strong language, and some adult and sexual content.)*

THE PLEDGE: Sean Penn's third directorial stint is his finest, providing Jack Nicholson with his best role in years. That's due in part to its source, a novel by Swiss writer Friedrich Dürrenmatt; vet film industry friends

Radley Metzger and Richard Gordon tell me the author scripted his own film adaptation in the early 1960s, which was released stateside as *It Happened in Broad Daylight* (*Es Geschah am Hellichten Tag*, 1958, US release 1960, starring Michel Simon and Gert Fröbe) to poor reviews and boxoffice. Unlike Penn's prior directing efforts, *The Indian Runner* (1991) and *The Crossing Guard* (1994), *The Pledge* doesn't simply set up a volatile scenario for his lead actors to grandstand within – it offers a somber, genuinely unsettling tale of an obsessed Nevada policeman (Nicholson) who can't let go of a horrific case of pedophilia and murder.

Sworn to the title pledge on the eve of his retirement by the mother of the eight-year-old victim, Nicholson alienates his former associates with his dogged pursuit of the phantom culprit on the thinnest of evidence. Buying a local gas stop, he puts down roots and patiently waits, eventually offering shelter to a battered mother (Robin Wright Penn) and daughter and become an affectionate caretaker. As it dawns on the viewer that something less savory might be perculating, the film eases into its tragic final act. Not a great film, but a very good one. Nicholson delivers a compelling performance in a vehicle worthy of his talents, and that's mighty rare of late. *(Rated 'R' for violence, strong adult and sexual content, strong language, and mature themes.)*

THE WEDDING PLANNER: This is not my cup of tea, but undemanding romantic comedy fans might find some fun here. True to formula, director Adam Shankman contrives to introduce titular wedding planner Mary Fiore (Jennifer Lopez) to literal life-saver Matthew McConaughey, only to keep them apart for the duration of the film. Lopez, of course, has dedicated herself to the marriages of others and is still single; when she falls for McConaughey, he's the groom in her all-important next big-ticket wedding. It's all a matter of time, you know, but I suppose that's the point; the entire confection exists to stretch the seemingly irreconcilable situation between these star-crossed lovers to the breaking point. I squirmed through every agonizing moment of the prolonged syrup, angst, and tedium; then again, I'm the guy who found a leech sucking Danny Masterson's eyelid amusing in *Dracula 2000*. My coworkers at the video store think it's *"cute."* God, how I hate *"cute." (Rated 'PG' for some adult and sexual content, language.)*

July 12:

SNATCH: Brit writer/director Guy Ritchie – who made a splash with his debut feature *Lock, Stock, and Two Smoking Barrels* in 1998, and makes another with his latest crime opus *Snatch* (2000) – is considered the Empire's answer to colonial upstart Quentin Tarantino (*Reservoir Dogs*, 1992, *Pulp Fiction*, 1994, *Jackie Brown*, 1997). I prefer to look at Ritchie's highly-entertaining black comedies in a wider cultural context.

Back in 1990, producer/director/star Warren Beatty mounted a completely skewed movie adaptation of Chester Gould's venerable comic strip *Dick Tracy*. As filmmakers so often do, Beatty played on the gaudy trappings of the strip (or, to be more specific, Gould's four-color Sunday strips) with garish, pop-art color decor and costumes, grotesque makeups, and simplistic dialogue. But aficionados of Gould's *Dick Tracy* – the comic strip, the *real* Dick Tracy – knew Beatty had gotten it all wrong: Gould's strip, in its heyday, was a perverse, dark, and hyper-violent morality play. In emulating the most superficial trappings of Gould's deceptively direct two-dimensional graphics, Beatty's *Dick Tracy* failed to capture the essence of the real *Dick Tracy*.

To my mind, Guy Ritchie *perfectly* translates Gould's dark universe to celluloid, with an ingratiating wit, vigor, and savagery guaranteed to put off the squeamish and faint-hearted. Though his anti-heroes live in polar opposition to Dick Tracy's rigid law & order position, Ritchie introduces us to a giddy rogue's gallery worthy of Gould's most outrageous creations with breathtaking immediacy.

Their names ring with bemusing Gouldian invention and intensity: Franky Four Fingers (Benicio Del Toro), Bullet-Tooth Tony (Vinnie Jones), drunken gypsy bare-knuckle boxer Mickey O'Neil (Brad Pitt), Russian mobster Boris the Blade (Rade Sherbedgia), crimelord Brick Top (Alan Ford), and our humble narrator Turkish (Jason Statham o*f Lock, Stock and Two Smoking Barrels*) and his hapless sidekick Tommy (Stephen Graham). While Beatty tried to translate the criminal grotesquery of Gould's strip to film with pounds of nifty Rick Baker latex makeups, Guy Ritchie cuts to the chase sans expensive trickery. Mickey O'Neil is a scruffy, scrappy Mumbles, his every word indecipherable to all but his Irish gypsy kin. Ritchie sustains Brick Top (the very name resonant of Tracy's infamous nemesis Flat Top) as a venomous monster with the pitch of his camera and Alan Ford's blunt delivery, looking for all the world like Albert Finney's bastard twin. With his eye inflated to cyclopean proportions by the lenses of his glasses as he casts one of his baleful sidelong glances, his words spit between worn, trap-like teeth as he consigns those he despises to hogchow for his prize swine, Brick Top is definitely a villain worthy of Chester Gould.

And nasty as it all sounds – and is – Ritchie keeps the pot boiling with break-neck pacing, giddy twists and turns, and irresistible black humor. The latter includes a hideous little dog with a penchant for swallowing found objects, including a squeeze toy that leaves it wheezing like a fugitive from *Toy Story* throughout.

The chain of events is triggered by thief and compulsive gambler Franky Four Fingers, stealing a diamond the size of the Ritz for Avi (Dennis Farina) via Avi's cousin Doug the Head (Mike Reid), who likes to present himself as a Jewish mogul. Enter Boris the Blade, whose set-up for Franky is undone by a hit on Boris' bookie operation by bumbling trio Vinney (Robbie Gee), Sol (Lennie James), and Tyrone (Ade). Meanwhile, nickel-and-dime boxing promoters Turkish and Tommy inadvertently cross the deadly Brick Top on a fixed fight, and have to hustle up a replacement fighter. Enter loco Mickey, a hard-drinking gypsy boxer with frightening stamina and a killer k.o. punch who may not choose to take the necessary dive in the fourth round. Lest we forget the diamond, Avi, unhappy with being left dangling in the breeze after Franky's disappearance, flies to London and engages the service of Bullet Tooth Tony to get his man and, more importantly, the stone.

Confused yet? The hell with it – take the ride. Though this certainly isn't everyone's cup of tea, I had a tremendous time with this flick. The accents may put off more viewers than the violence; having many friends in the UK, north to south, I didn't have a stitch of trouble, and even understood Mickey's inspired Irish Mumbles pastiche (which scares me a bit, really), but I'm told by many they had a tough time, so there ya go. You've been warned. The cast is excellent, and even golden-boy Pitt (who was so painful to watch in *The Mexican*, 2001, coming to home video later in the summer) plays one of his best roles for all it's worth, submerging himself like a chameleon into the fringe underbelly as if he was born to it. For fans of *Lock, Stock, and Two Smoking Barrels* and *The Boondock Saints* (1999) – you know who you are – *Snatch* is the summer's best video to date. Recommended! *(Rated 'R' for strong language, adult situations, nudity, and extreme violence.)*

YOU CAN COUNT ON ME: Worlds away from Guy Ritchie's punchdrunk universe is writer/director Kenneth Lonergan's marvelous *You Can Count on Me* (2000), which I am loathe to praise too highly for fear of building unrealistic expectations. This, too, is one of the summer's best video releases, and among the most understated but potent dramas of this or any season. Where Ritchie's film is driven by almost cartoony kinetics, mayhem, and cinematic flourishes, Lonergan eases us into his characters and their lives with grace and quiet observation. The way, and times, that eyes do or don't meet, softly asserting the heartfelt ties and unspoken betrayals over the years, lend *You Can Count on Me* a novelistic depth and the flavor of lives experienced as they are lived.

This is a rare, meditative, and truly adult pleasure amid the clang and clamor of the theatrical summer season, and one to be savored.

Orphaned at tender ages by an unfortunate car accident, older sister Sammy (Laura Linney) shares a strong bond with her wayward younger brother Terry (Mark Ruffalo) that is tested by an unexpected, but welcome, visit to Sammy's upstate New York home. As a single mother raising her own young boy, eight-year-old Rudy (Rory Culkin – yes, brother to that other Culkin lad),

Sammy inevitably rankles at Terry's nomadic wandering and troubled baggage. He's left behind a suicidal pregnant girlfriend and confesses to having just finished a jail sentence, compounding his ongoing problems with drugs, lowlife companions, tangles with the law, and emotional instability. But Terry sees through Sammy's moral posturing, too, simultaneously smirking at her own infidelities (a sexual fling with her incompetent new bank boss Brian, played with self-effacing skill by Matthew Broderick) while accepting fully such lapses as part of being human. She was, Terry hints to Rudy at their first dinner together, a real 'wild child,' and we come to see the truth of this as Sammy struggles to keep her own footing between marital proposals from her semi-steady (Jon Tenney) and steamy motel meetings with Brian. Sammy counters with a visit from the local priest to counsel Terry; typical of the film's many virtues, writer/director Lonergan eschews the melodramatic potential of the confrontation to capture a quieter, richer, deeper exchange. Nevertheless, the narrative does arrive at far more volatile emotional turf when Terry chooses to drive Rudy to meet the father he has never met, bringing Lonergan's tale to its climax.

In an era in which politicians still spout piously about 'family values' – as if there were some never-never land behind or ahead of us in which domestic bliss were more than a fantasy, and emotional relationships were somehow free of baggage, burdens, and the hard work they require each and every day – *You Can Count on Me* is a most welcome breath of fresh air. Laura Linney and Mark Ruffalo inhabit their characters and create a chemistry unlike any I've seen in years, illuminating countless corners of sibling exile and love, loyalty and rivalry, joys tasted and agonies shared. This is, on its own terms, an excellent film, and not to be missed. *(Rated 'R' for strong language, adult and sexual situations, nudity, casual drug and alcohol use and abuse, and interpersonal violence.)*

July 20:

THE GIFT: Multi-talented Billy Bob Thornton – the actor, writer, and director of *Sling Blade* (1996) who most recently directed *All the Pretty Horses* (2000)[25] – collaborated with co-scripter Tom Epperson to craft this thick slice of Southern Gothic, resonantly tapping the supernatural vein of last season's *The Sixth Sense* and *A Stir of Echoes*.[26] Though it isn't quite up to the high standards of authors like Flannery O'Connor or the lesser-known novelist Davis Grubb (*Night of the Hunter*, etc.), or the cinematic power of my all-time favorite psychic thriller *Don't Look Now* (directed by Nicolas Roeg, 1973, from a story by Daphne DuMaurier), *The Gift* is a potent summer shocker. Sure to illicit a chill or two en route to the resolution of its central murder mystery, the real drawing card here is the top-drawer ensemble cast, who inhabit their roles with contagious conviction.

The somber proceedings begin with an unnerving portrait of the day-to-day life of Brixton, Georgia widow Annie Wilson (Cate Blanchett). Struggling in the wake of her husband's untimely death, Annie ekes out an impoverished living for herself and her three young sons by doing 'readings' for the locals, applying her very real psychic abilities to their various issues, concerns, and

---

[25] See this volume, p. 27.
[26] See *Blur, Vol. 1*, pp. 192-194, 250-252.

complaints as best she can. But life in Brixton is fraught with peril, and we quickly see that Annie's livelihood exposes her to shockingly intimate eruptions of personalized, emotional, and domestic violence. A consultation with a beaten housewife (Hilary Swank of *Boys Don't Cry*, 1999[27]) prompts her abusive husband (Keanu Reeves) to tear into the Wilson household, threatening mother and offspring; a stuttering young garage mechanic (Giovanni Ribisi) plagued by an unspeakable dread of what he might do when he looks into *"a blue diamond"* appeals for more aid than Annie seems capable of providing, and explodes into furious rages with the smallest provocation. Amid this steaming gumbo of festering emotions, the sudden disappearance of upscale socialite Jessica (Katie Holmes) and the eve of her wedding to the well-respected school principal (Greg Kinnear) plunges Annie into increasingly disturbing visions of Jessica's fate and escalating confrontations with friend and foe alike.

As already noted, the players are uniformly excellent, lead by Cate Blanchett (who left her indelible mark with the lead role in *Elizabeth*, 1998). She infuses Annie with a heartbreaking, stoic blend of warmth, dignity, and strength. The biggest surprise here, though, is director Sam Raimi's skill as an actor's director; his *mise en scène* is as evocative as ever, thick with fog, Spanish moss, and the high whine of cicadas, but Raimi's deft orchestration of the performers is remarkable. This is the man who made his mark with high-octane splatterfests *The Evil Dead* (1983) and *Evil Dead 2* (1987) before his Hollywood breakthroughs with energetic pulp like *Darkman* (1990) and *The Quick and the Dead* (1994),

---

[27] See *Blur, Vol. 2*, pp. 44-46, and *Blur, Vol. 3*, pp. 82-83.

and producing popcorn TV series *Hercules: The Legendary Journeys* (1995-99) and *Xena: Warrior Princess* (1995-2001). Raimi's most mature work to date remains *A Simple Plan* (1998), which none-too-coincidentally co-starred Billy Bob Thornton as the simple-minded participant in theft and murder who crumbled under the moral weight of his role in such crimes. Thornton and Raimi are a compelling team here as well, with both running the show from behind the camera. Though the narrative twists and turns of *The Gift* show wear before the final act, this is an effective chiller with far richer characterizations – and prompting more late-night reveries – than you might expect. *(Rated 'R' for violence, gore, nudity, adult and sexual situations, and strong language.)*

THIRTEEN DAYS: In the wake of the notorious Bay of Pigs fiasco, President John F. Kennedy faced his greatest national crisis in October, 1962. Military intelligence aerial photography of Cuba revealed the presence of covert Russian ballistic missile bases being established in Cuba, which would present a significant threat to the continental U.S. in a mere thirteen days.

For *Thirteen Days* (2001), director Roger Donaldson (who previously collaborated with star Kevin Costner on the thriller *No Way Out*, 1987) and screenwriter David Self distill the essence of the Cuban missile crisis into a literate, intelligent, and taut suspenser. Literally under the gun, President Kennedy (Bruce Greenwood) negotiates the political gauntlet in hopes of averting nuclear Armageddon, pressured by the military brass to strike first while cautious cabinet members and counsels seek diplomatic solutions against ever-mounting odds stacked against peaceful settlement. Kennedy is not alone: crucial participants include brother and Attorney General Robert F. Kennedy (Steven Culp) – author of the book *Thirteen Days: A Memoir of the Cuban Missile Crisis* that inspired the film (along with Ernest R. May and Philip D. Zelikow's *The Kennedy Tapes: Inside the White House During the Cuban Missile Crisis*).

Self and Donaldson also position Special Assistant to the President Kenneth O'Donnell (Kevin Costner) as the film's nominal witness and everyman hero, a ploy that put off some critics but worked pretty well for me, though Costner's mock-Bostonian accent does grate on the nerves now and again. That caveat aside, *Thirteen Days* is a fine piece of work, sparked with sharp performances, succinct scripting, and efficient direction throughout, anchored by a riveting sense of time and place, and the courage of its convictions.

The DVD presentation is particularly noteworthy, introducing New Line Home Entertainment's ambitious *"InfiniFilm"* format. Building on the 'white rabbit' feature of *The Matrix* (1999) DVD,[28] the *Thirteen Days* DVD allows the viewer to re-view the film with 'footnotes': running cues at the bottom of the screen that allow one to detour from specific scenes into relevant 'extras' (historical archival footage, interviews with historians, witnesses, and participants detailing the events fictionalized in the feature itself, filmographies, or behind-the-scenes production tidbits) before returning to the film without missing a narrative beat. Teachers, take note! Individually, these *"InfiniFilm"* 'factoids' run from 20 seconds to a little over three minutes each, adding over two hours – and considerable depth and context – to the total viewing experience. This adds immeasura-

---

[28] See *Blur, Vol. 1*, pp. 51-53.

bly to a historical docudrama like *Thirteen Days*, particularly when one is able to sample commentary by none other than Sergei Khrushchev (son of Soviet Union leader Nikita) offering insights to the Russian side of the Crisis.

Though the *"InfiniFilm"* format might be of dubious merit when applied to a less worthy film (such as New Line's next *"InfiniFilm"* DVD feature *15 Minutes*, coming later this summer), this is an ideal addendum to *Thirteen Days*, though I do urge you to watch the film uninterrupted first. It's a crackling drama well worth your attention, engaging and rewarding on its own terms sans the DVD bells and whistles. Recommended. *(Rated 'PG-13' for strong language.)*

July 26:

Here's the first of two mid-summer catch-up columns. There's been far, far too many new releases for me to even begin to stay on top of the torrent. So bear with me a couple of weeks as I blitz through the seasonal video harvest.

A special note for those who care: despite frequent announcements in various video columns and sources, Wong Kar-Wai's delicate *In the Mood for Love* (*Fa Yeung Nin Wa*, 2000) has been delayed. It finally streets on July 31st. Patience. Wong Kar-Wai [29] would want you to be patient.

---

[29] Kar Wai Wong has become the preferred name; at the time this column was written, it was Wong Kar-Wai in most American venues.

THE CAVEMAN'S VALENTINE: Samuel L. Jackson rightly plays center-stage as a homeless Juilliard-trained prodigy who dwells in a park cavern and watches shows only he can see on his unplugged TV set (ah, finally, an alternative to cable and satellite; there's never anything on anyway!). Prone to schizo delusions (vividly depicted for the viewer) of an omnipresent, omnipotent corporate-kingpin Moriarty responsible for all perceived evils, Jackson is wrenched into a reality of sorts when a street kid's corpse is found propped in a tree outside his Flintstones doorway. He's drawn into solving the convoluted mystery behind the teenager's brutal death, and we're dragged along for the often psychedelic ride.

Director Kasi Lemmons, who previously collaborated with Jackson for her stunning debut feature *Eve's Bayou* (1997), milks the premise and performances for all they're worth, and Jackson is never less than riveting every step of the way. The underrated Colm Feore (*32 Short Films about Glenn Gould*, 1993, *Storm of the Century*, 1999, etc.) is once again the calm, insidious center of a cyclone here as the photographic provocateur whose sadomasochistic creations lurk at the black heart of the crime. I quite enjoyed this curio, though its entrancingly fragmented 'who-dun-what' stylistic conceits were promptly eclipsed by the far more inventive, intoxicating plunge of *Memento* (2000, coming this fall to home video, and worth the wait). Nevertheless, give the *Caveman* a visit. *(Rated 'R')*

CITY ON FIRE: Quentin Tarantino fans, *Reservoir Dogs* lovers, take note: *this* is the Hong Kong crime caper that Tarantino plundered for his bracing 1992 directorial debut. Ringo Lam's engaging *City on Fire* (*Lung Fu Fong Wan*, 1987) was the source for many of *Reser-*

voir Dogs's devilish delights, and it's finally in video stores everywhere – draw your own conclusions. Hong Kong buffs will also savor the team-up of Chow Yun-Fat and Danny Lee, herein establishing the chemistry that John Woo tapped for his classic *The Killer* (*Dip Huet Seung Hung*, 1990). Though it seems a bit tame in light of the Woo hyper-kinetics and snappy Tarantino ratchet-job and patter that followed in its footsteps, *City on Fire* is still an entertaining suspenser that builds to a rousing final act – just remember, though. The deja-vu you're experiencing is misplaced. Check it out! *(Rated 'R')*

THE FAMILY MAN: Afraid of commitment? Scaling the heights of career climbing? No time for lovey-dovey beyond the 'wham-bam-thank-you-madame' scene? Jack Campbell (Nicolas Cage) is there, until a coy street angel (Don Cheadle, above this sort of thing) gives Jack a taste – a loooooong taste – of the life he left behind when he left his college sweetheart Kate (Tea Leoni, in a somewhat more substantial role than her thankless turn in this summer's *Jurassic Park III* provides) at the airport. The film aspires to be a romantic mid-life crisis wake-up call ala Frank Capra's *It's A Wonderful Life* (1946), but it's actually a companion piece to the peculiar female 'what if?' genre embodied by *Peggy Sue Got Married* (1986, which Cage also co-starred in), *Sliding Doors* (1997), *Passion of Mind* (2000),[30] etc. In fact, *The Family Man* is the male appropriation (read: remake) of the much more compelling *My Myself I* (1999),[31] in which Rachel Griffiths carried the day with her excellent performance

---

[30] See *Blur, Vol. 3*, pp. 16, 115.
[31] See *Blur, Vol. 3*, pp. 16, 115.

in the role essayed by Cage here. Whatever substance Griffiths brought to *Me Myself I* is here melted down into sugar-on-snow amid the New Jersey wasteland. This wish fulfillment fantasy will endear itself to those of you drawn to such fare, though it will wear out its welcome for many before the finale. *(Rated 'PG-13')*

SWEET NOVEMBER: For tearjerker lovers only. Here's a completely unnecessary, who-asked-for-it remake of the never-on-video (so don't ask)[32] 1968 romance staring Sandy Dennis and Anthony Newley: in that forgotten oddity, she wooed a different man every month to boost the confidence of her timid suitors before sending them on their way, until Newley insists on marrying her. For reasons only known in Hollywood, enough Los Angeles execs thought that premise was just crying out for the Millennial retread, matchmaking fickle, fragile Charlize Theron with vain, vapid Keanu Reeves except – oh, darn. She has a terminal illness. Who'da thunk it. She squanders her time, and so have I; you shouldn't. I, at least, got paid a wee bit to write this column. *(Rated 'PG-13')*

VALENTINE: Regular readers of this column know I do love a good horror movie, and quite a few bad ones, too. This clinker is superior to the *Urban Legends* duo by a single monkey hair's judgment, but don't let that fool you. It's a stinker, not a howler, and hence no fun. Fans of the TV series *Angel* can give this wide berth, despite the lead presence of TV hunk David Boreanaz (looking a little thick around the neck here).

---

[32] Actually, Warner Home Video *did* issue the 1968 *Sweet November* – on vhs only – in 2001.

After the obligatory 1980s slasher film opener detailing a high-school humiliation sure to trigger retribution, a braindead clutch of coiffed babes (Jessica Capshaw, Jessica Cauffiel, Katherine Heigl, and Denise Richards in her latest phone-it-in role) receive the titular valentines sweetening the usual heartfelt devotions with promises of carnage. They are unceremoniously plucked like flower petals, violently (but not too violent – this is, after all, a sterile 'R' horror movie) snuffed, one by one. But, like, they can't interrupt their vacuous lifestyles and endless back-biting partying long enough to kick into survivor mode. Knock 'em dead, Romeo.

One male lap-dog idiot ends up tied down in bed after making lewd and crude moves on Denise, who pouts and poses before making creative use of a candle to leave the sap scarred for life and strung out for further gory plucking. Alas, the film never, ever lets us know his fate. Did he untie himself in time for another keg tapping? Did the baby-masked nose-bleeding killer perform a long-overdue religious ritual on the fellow? This, alone, left me chewing thoughtfully on my popcorn kernels long after the rest of the film had evaporated from memory. Like, two seconds into the credits.

You want my advice? Stick with *The Caveman's Valentine*. He, at least, loves you. *(Rated 'R')*

August 2:

The mid-summer overview of new and recent video releases continues with this round-up of post-apocalyptic cyber-punk bikers and mad artists. As I mentioned last week, it's been almost impossible to keep up with the flood of new and remastered titles on video, so it's catch-up time!

AKIRA: Katsuhiro Otomo's breakthrough 1988 science-fiction anime classic hits the new release shelves in a sterling remastered edition;[33] if you've never seen *Akira*, now's the time. Otomo's lively tale of biker-gang warfare in futuristic Neo-Tokyo is still a corker, depicting the clash of super-science and military power as a resurrected legacy of genetic mutation spawns a race of telekinetic super-children, threatening to topple the metropolis into another apocalypse of almost unimaginable proportions. Though it fumbles in its final act, *Akira* is still a masterpiece (Otomo finished the film before he had completed his truly epic, multi-volume 'manga' novel – currently available in English from Dark Horse Comics – leaving a few too many loose conceptual ends in the feature's daunting condensation of the manga's sprawling scope). This is the film that justifiably awakened the world to the visionary potential of the Japanese anime, and stands as a true landmark in animation and cinema. Otomo's staging of action and rich characterizations is equally potent (though the female characters unfortunately get short shrift), the visuals are intoxicating and often devastating in their vivid power, and Geinoh Yamashirogumi's musical score is an absolute masterpiece. The double-disc DVD Collector's Edition offers an incredible treasure-trove of riches (if you want to buy it, don't wait – it's already slipping out-of-print!), with more extras than even the most rabid *Akira* junkie can absorb in a single sitting. Not to be missed! *(Unrated, but would most likely earn an 'R' rating for violence.)*

---

[33] See *Blur, Vol. 1*, pp. 214, 216, 217.

THE BODY: What a premise: an archeological dig in Israel, beneath a shop owned by a Palestinian, uncovers what might be the remains of Jesus Christ Himself. If Christ wasn't resurrected, whither Christianity? The Vatican dispatches priest and ex-soldier Antonio Banderas to investigate. He clashes with the Jewish archaeologist who made the discovery (Olivia Williams), the inevitable opportunistic Israeli-Palestinian conflicts over the mysterious dig site, and agonizes over his verdict that could spear the very heart of the Church and all Christiandom. Writer-director Jonas McCord knows he's got a tiger by the tail, but he loses his grip despite a stellar cast (particularly Banderas, Williams, and co-star Derek Jacobi). Simply put, McCord isn't up to the heady challenge of such heresy. Cinematically, he fails to even fetishize that which threatens to topple the faith of millions, thus dissipating the very heart of his conceit. Thanks to its cast, this curious, compelling, misbegotten medium-budget Hollywood-Euro companion to the current Christian filmmaking movement (*The Omega Code, Left Behind: The Movie, The Judgment*, etc.)[34] rewards a look, unless you find its very concept offensive. (Rated 'PG-13')

DOWN TO EARTH: Chris Rock is engaging, but little else is in this dreary revamp of Harry Segall's venerable fantasy play, already adapted to the screen as *Here Comes Mr. Jordan* (1941), *Down to Earth* (1947, a musical version starring Rita Hayworth), and the stylish, witty Warren Beatty/Buck Henry remake *Heaven Can Wait* (1978). No style or wit on view here. Rock is Lance Barton, bicycle messenger by day, grating stand-up comic

---

[34] See *Blur, Vol. 1*, pp. 243-250.

by night. When an accident sends him to his unscheduled death, the angelic Mr. King (Chazz Palminteri) and Mr. Keyes (Eugene Levy, offering the film's brightest performance) scramble to find Lance a new body for the interim. He lands in the husk of wealthy elderly white bigot Charles Wellington, falls for lovely activist Sontee (Regina King), and so it goes. The biggest problem is the film's schizo playing of Rock as Wellington – Sontee clearly falls for Rock, who is often shown on-screen, but we're supposed to think she's actually interacting with a rich Caucasian wheezer, a ruse the maladroit filmmakers completely fumble – and Lance is supposed to be a bad comedian, further squandering Rock's true forte. What were they thinking? For diehard Rock fans only, who are sure to be disappointed. *(Rated 'PG-13')*

MONKEYBONE: More afterlife foolishness and body-switching figures in Henry Selick's *Monkeybone* (2001), which is at least a more original concoction. Brendan Fraser stars as mild-mannered cartoonist Stu Miley, overwhelmed by the unexpected media success of his lewd, crude creation *Monkeybone*, a cartoon primate that embodies an uncontrollable part of his anatomy and functions as his obscene 'Mr. Hyde' alter-ego (voiced by John Turturro). Monkeybone is an unlikely media darling, to say the least; clearly, this is the film's surrogate for the gross-out cartoon celebrity savored by *Ren & Stimpy, Beavis & Butthead*, and *South Park*'s crew of foul-mouthed mites.

Stu loathes the limelight and proposed product lines his agent foists upon him for approval; the latter prove deadly when an oversized inflatable Monkeybone sends Stu and his fiance Julie (Bridget Fonda) careening into a freak car accident, plunging Stu into a vegetative coma state. Stu awakens in 'Downtown,' a carnivalesque nightmare netherworld populated by the discards of our collective id – including (Ta-*da!*) Monkeybone himself. In the ensuing shenanigans, Stu and Monkeybone steal a Willy Wonka-like golden 'exit pass' back to reality. However, only one of them can inhabit Stu's flesh-and-blood body; Monkeybone mutinies, stealing Stu's mortal coil to horn in on life with Julie (and orchestrate a proliferation of nightmares to 'feed' his Downtown cronies), leaving Stu to stew and plan his own escape.

Director Henry Selick (*James and the Giant Peach*, 1996) mounts a delirious but muddled fantasy. Still stuck in the shadow of his collaboration with Tim Burton on *The Nightmare Before Christmas* (1993), Selick's latest comes off as a murky variation on Burton's *Beetlejuice* (1988). Selick cooks up an eclectic visual banquet, but his dubious storytelling skills are taxed by the film's patchwork script and multiple realities. At its best, *Monkeybone* offers fleeting tidbits of dark comedy (including Joe Camel's cameo in Downtown) and truly disturbing imagery (one sequence, in which a carrot-like Stu writhes beneath the scalpel of a monstrous surgeon, is unlike anything ever seen in a major studio production, evoking the outrageous visionary art of *outré* painters Robert Williams and Alan Clarke). At its worst, the film is an uneasy wedding of sitcom silliness, overblown comedy-action setpieces, and romantic naivete.

The DVD offers some fascinating insights into the ambitious wedding of stop-motion model animation, live effects, and CGI, and how Kaja Blackley and Vanessa Chong's graphic novel *Dark Town* (1995, Mad Monkey Press; in which a comatose puppeteer found himself trapped in a nether realm of ambulatory puppets) was transmuted into *Monkeybone*. The director commentary track is surprisingly candid about Selick's unhappy creative relations with Chris Columbus (director of *Home Alone,* 1990, *Bicentennial Man*, 1999, etc.) and parent studio 20th Century Fox. I can't really recommend the film, but it's better than *Down to Earth* for its shaggy-dog misanthropy and bizarre flights of fancy. Fellow mutants will find much to savor here among the shambles. *(Rated 'PG-13'; definitely not for young children!)*

SAVING SILVERMAN: This misogynist, moronic comedy manages to make even Jack Black (*High Fidelity*, *Tenacious D*, etc.) wear out his welcome. Lame musician Silverman (the singularly unappealing Jason Biggs of *American Pie*) falls for psychologist girlfriend (Amanda Peet), and lamer musician confederates J.D. (Jack Black) and Wayne (Steve Zahn, who somehow retains his dignity even here) decide it's their mission to, well, you know: *Save Silverman*. Save your shekels; what an embarrassment. Sophomoric idiocy for first-week freshmen only; don't fret, though, the soon-to-home-video travesty *Tomcats* is an even more excruciating entry in this season's young-male-sexist-pigs-laff-fest sweepstakes. *(Rated 'PG-13')*

August 9-16: For Love of Cinema

Making my way through yet more of the mid-summer harvest of new video releases, I can't help but wonder what draws customers, like moths, to the bright lights of the so-called 'hits.'

I also have to wonder what prompts me to write about it, week after week.

I know what attracts me: I'm in it for the love of cinema, the love of movies. I look for movies to take me places – real and imaginary places, emotional spaces, dream and nightmare environments – I cannot, will not, or would not go to in my waking life. I love the uppers and downers, and the more extreme the ascent or descent, the better.

This appetite encompasses almost anything, really, from what some find appealing to what many find appalling. There's nothing elitist about it, mind you. Among my favorite summer theatrical experiences thus far were *Shrek* (the ultimate *Fractured Fairy Tale*) and *Jurassic Park III* (kept the ten-year-old dinosaur freak in me happy enough to keep the weary 46-year-old within addled), and I quite enjoyed seeing *Songcatcher* this past weekend, which sweetens a formulaic romance with its enchanting flirtation with North Carolina mountain folk and music.

But the summer viewing experiences that have mattered most to me are utterly alien to most moviegoers. I completely enjoyed a collection of short films by local filmmakers shown last weekend up in Bellows Falls. I've been catching up on Walter Ungerer's somber 1970s features like *The Animal* (1976) and *The House Without Steps* (1979), and wonder how I missed seeing them before. Then there was the privileged preview of Michel Moyse's just-completed duo-screen video feature *Cowards* (which still haunts me); Tsui Hark's giddy high-octane Hong Kong/Chinese crime flick *Time and Tide* (*Senulau Ngaklau*, 2000); the recent (apparently illegal) DVD crop of dubbed, black-and-white Mexican horror movies made in the early 1960s, including the almost surreal *The Brainiac* (*El Barón del Terror*, 1962); the steady flow of gorgeous letterboxed, fully-restored

DVD editions of Italian director Mario Bava's colorful low-budget marvels. I loved every second of these, and yet could not write about them here because there was the urgency of yet another week of 'hot new releases' to write about instead. Who among you cares about the delights of the restored 1925 *The Lost World* [35] or the revelations of the original Italian cut of Bava's portmanteau *Black Sabbath* (*I Tre Volti Della Paura*, 1963) when *Cast Away* fills every video rental and retail shelf from sea to shining sea to overflow?

Even a casual weekly assessment of what does and does not fly off the new release wall in our own video store offers constant evidence of the eccentricities of my own appetite. Judging by the wall, most of our customers love the kind of movies that aren't really movies, to my mind.

This week, for instance, we have **THE MEXICAN** (2001) and **3000 MILES TO GRACELAND** (2001). To my mind, these are 'movies' that literally do... not... move. They thrash around and make a lot of noise, but they are inert, in that they don't take me anywhere. They just eat up time. That they do so relatively harmlessly may be part of the allure: 'Movies' as narcotic, as pacifiers, Hollywood star-vehicles as empty and superficially tasty/tasteless as the popcorn we shovel down and colored carbonated water we gulp while viewing them. They barely tell stories at all. They are package deals, pure and simple, the wet-dreams of agents, producers, and uncritical fans of the stars who are happy to drink in that spectacle however empty the receptacle.

---

[35] See my exhaustive article on the restored 1925 *The Lost World* in *Video Watchdog* #75, September 2001, pp. 22-45.

The Mexican pretends to be about the titular rare pistol that threatens to divide a strained relationship between lovers Julia Roberts and Brad Pitt, but it really isn't about anything more than what a sweet package it is to slap Roberts and Pitt together for a little over two hours. There's absolutely nothing to chew on here (effortlessly-attractive Roberts and Pitt can't even muster enough sparks between them to chew the scenery, despite all the huffing and puffing), so the package is beefed up a bit by the inclusion of James Gandolfini (Tony Soprano himself). Gandolfini lends some spam to this coy white-bread mix of mock-Tarantino 'edginess' and pirated South of the Border Sam Peckinpah theatrics (as if the long-dead director of savage masterpieces like *The Wild Bunch*, 1969, *Straw Dogs*, 1971, and *Bring Me the Head of Alfredo Garcia*, 1974, were another flavorful spice to pinch and add to 'the package'). But it is spam spread between two thin pieces of Wonder Bread, and I just can't work up any enthusiasm over it. I can't even hate it. It isn't worth the juice.

3000 Miles to Graceland is somehow more alluring, and even more vapid. A dream cast (Kevin Costner, Kurt Russell, etc.) dolled up as Elvis impersonators rob $3 mil from a Las Vegas casino. Of course, it all blows up in their (and our) faces. Another former music video director, Demian Lichtenstein, robs pop iconography as shamelessly as his pop-artist namesake did in the 1950s, to little or no effect. Despite the chic Elvisness of it all, the relentless pyrotechnics, the vicious R-rated splatter and mayhem, it's a yawn-fest. The only perverse pleasure here is seeing Kurt Russell in Elvis gear two decades after he starred in the made-for-TV *Elvis* (1979, directed by John Carpenter of 1978 *Halloween* fame); a kick for some of us, but nothing to wrap a recommendation around. Again, the only excitement here was for the agents who put this 'dream team' together for this 'dream pic' – leaving nothing but the bones of a maybe-movie for a weary viewer to discard.

Even the high-end of the week's new releases, multi-Academy Award nominee ***CHOCOLAT*** (2000), is a 'package deal,' and as such highly suspect.

A little history lesson: prior to being bought up by Disney a few years ago, distributor Miramax was a scrappy newcomer, building their reputation on scrappy domestic independent films and volatile imports (like Peter Greenaway's *The Cook, The Thief, His Wife and Her Lover*, 1989). Throughout the 1990s, Miramax nurtured audiences with alternatives to the big-studio blockbusters, and in doing so wooed profits and Oscars for foreign fare like *Cinema Paradiso* (1988) and *Life is Beautiful* (1997), while learning the art of packaging their own 'imports.' Two of these, *The English Patient* (1996) and *Shakespeare in Love* (1998), won Best Picture Oscars. With *Chocolat*, one sees Miramax's current formula for creating its own distinctive brand of audience-friendly, *faux*-French films. However seductive the result, one cannot help but shake the feeling that this is, after all, a confection. It's a pleasant, soothing confection, but a confection nonetheless.

Mix one currently popular French actress, Juliette Binoche (and a cameo from the venerable Leslie Caron), with three parts international flavoring (a melange of accents from Judi Dench, Alfred Molina, Lena Olin) and one part American alternative star (Johnny Depp, flourishing a bohemian Irish-gypsy persona). Blend with restless romance and a simplistic homily on diversity vs. provincial intolerance set in a quaint French village. Fold ingredients and stir. Bake under the sure directorial hand of Scandinavian chocolate-chef extraordinaire Lasse Hallström, who made his mark with *My Life as a Dog* (1987), back in the kitchen on the heels of his successful adaptation of John Irving's *The Cider House Rules* (1999). Cool and release *sans* the need for distressing subtitles; serve to the masses. Serves millions.

Chocolat is a very seductive piece, lovingly prepared and catering to the distinctive palettes of 'discerning' alternative and foreign film audiences. I, too, fell under its spell, and quite enjoyed myself, all the while knowing I was watching what can only be called a 'prefab French film.' *"What a sap I am,"* I thought, as I adored the flavor and delicious aftertaste. It is, in a way, a perfect solution to the diminishing returns of Hollywood remakes of successful foreign films (usually losing the key elements in the 'translation'): *pre*-make successful faux-foreign films for the target audience, filming in English.

The fact that such a succinctly pleasing sweet can be manufactured for an audience that prides itself on a taste for alternative and foreign films demonstrates that they – we (myself included) – do not harbor such a rarefied or distinctive palette after all. Miramax has calculated, with surgical precision, how to titillate the 'alternative' taste buds, and do so here with singular, shameless hucksterism. Here we are, a generation of Truffaut, Kurosawa, and Bergman aficionados, played like rubes at the carny. *Chocolat* shamelessly plays to all its projected audience's shared liberal presumptions, fears, prejudices (Molina's Comte de Reynaud tidily embodies them all), fancies, dreams, and aspirations. Let's not forget, after all, that the entire foreign film industry in America was built on the exploitative potential of the pleasures of the flesh, its bedrock laid by Brigitte Bardot imports that promised glimpses of skin once forbidden by Hollywood. The pleasures of the flesh are likewise central to *Chocolat*, though its brand of exploitation is a bit less sensationalistic than that practiced in the 1950s.

Like the intoxicating substance it derives its title from, *Chocolat* melts in your mouth and tastes great – but I know it's eating at my teeth. I need my choppers for something of substance, something worth chewing on.

So, what's the problem? As my friend Elizabeth Monteleone noted in her letter to me about *Chocolat*, I'm picking on a very enjoyable movie. Elizabeth responds, *"at least Johnny Depp (very seductive with his non-conformist persona – he's the bad boy we 'good' girls love) brings a sort of 'smartness' to the roles many writers lovingly create. I loved* Chocolat *precisely because it was a mushy movie full of romance. Really good romance movies with smart women are hard to come by."* (Friend and veteran director Radley Metzger writes, *"Have you heard they are remaking* Chocolat *on a very low budget in digital video? It's called* Carob.*"*)[36]

Well, yes, Elizabeth, you're right. I, too, enjoyed *Chocolat*, and can (and did) recommend it. I enjoyed it as much as I did ***ENEMY AT THE GATES*** (2001), another continental (and formulaic) affair, an epic west-

---

[36] Quoted, with permission during initial *Video Views* publication, from emails from Elizabeth Monteleone and Radley Metzger, August 2001. Elizabeth and Radley were among the circle of friends I emailed the weekly column to upon completion – the friends & family email distribution of *Video Views* that evolved (or devolved) into my daily blog of 2005+. Also note my wife Marjory – then my fiancé – was in complete agreement with Elizabeth; *Chocolat* is among Marge's favorite films.

ern disguised as a war film, exquisitely crafted by French director Jean-Jacques Annaud (*Quest for Fire/La Guerre du Feu*, 1981, *The Name of the Rose/Der Name der Rose*, 1986, *The Bear/L'Ours*, 1988, *The Lover/L'Amant*, 1992, *Seven Years in Tibet*, 1997, etc.) for domestic and international audiences.

I've always enjoyed Annaud's films. *Enemy at the Gates* boasts a sterling cast (Jude Law, Joseph Fiennes, Ed Harris, Bob Hoskins, and Rachel Weisz), an arresting historical canvas (World War 2's Russian front), and a riveting scenario extrapolated from a genuine life-and-death confrontation between snipers who were national heroes in their respective armies. Thus, the classical western 'showdown' narrative is pitched into a vivid wartime arena, and Annaud squeezes every drop of mud-caked, blood-and-brain spattered suspense possible from the contrast of intimately personal, versus propagandistic political, loyalties and betrayals.

The western elements are further embodied in Jude Law's rugged, reluctant every man hero, who attracts the unwelcome attention of Ed Harris's Nazi veteran sharpshooter. Harris is determined to take down the young upstart who has so shaken the Third Reich war machine, and he moves with an uncanny reptilian opacity and calm to achieve that goal. The spectacle is mesmerizing, fusing rousing setpieces (the siege of Stalingrad) with quiet confrontations worthy of Sergio Leone's operatic westerns.

All in all, it's as intelligent and compelling as *Chocolat*. Both films are perfectly tuned to the needs and nuances of their respective genres – and that, my friend, sums up their virtues and weaknesses.

Galvanizing as Ed Harris is in *Enemy at the Gates*, he clearly poured more of himself into his true labor of love, ***POLLOCK*** (2001), and you can feel the heat in every frame. That *heat* is what keeps me going as a viewer: I crave it, hunger for it, and when I find it, I treasure it.

Thus, the point of this ramble: I inevitably find more to savor in the works of passion than I do in the slickest 'packaged' movies, however alluring the package, diverting the elements, or fine-tuned the precision polish.

Labors of love are often ragged, groping, ungainly affairs: sweaty, messy, and painfully raw. Such is the case with *Pollock*, which peers into the abyss with unflinching masochistic abandon without satisfactorily unveiling (or arriving at) the heart of its subject. By comparison, *Chocolat* and *Enemy at the Gates* are far more satisfying entertainments, sumptuously mounted and beautifully realized, neatly tying up all their narrative threads in their final moments. But *Pollock* radiates the heat *Chocolat* and *Enemy at the Gates* only approach, and has has stayed with me long after their pleasures faded. Though it *"fails"* as an entertainment (which it does not intend to be), as a movie *Pollock* moved me in unexpected ways, and I can't shake it's wake.

Pollock is a flawed work, but it is the honest expression of a great actor's genuine obsessions: a rare commodity in this summer's video harvest. Ed Harris stars as pioneer modern painter Jackson Pollock in this bleak, often scathing biopic that revels without apology in the artist's volatile creativity and rage. Harris' decade-long obsession with this production prompted him to rise to the challenge to make this his directorial debut, too, and it's a stunning maiden voyage – true to Harris' best work as a performer, oddly mirroring his screen debut in George Romero's marvelous, sadly underrated

Knightriders (1981), in which he starred as another self-possessed, self-destructive visionary.

Pollock was (in the words of an art historian interviewed for the *Pollock* DVD's extra features) *"the James Dean of the art world,"* and the film lives up to that legacy. As Pollock, Harris is believably shy and tentative, wary of human contact; insatiable in his sexual appetites, volcanic in his emotions; and, as Pollock moves from the constraints of his early work to embrace the freedom of moving from tube to liquid paint, from the easel to the floor, in a progression of expansive canvases, Harris moves like a dancer driven by uncanny internal rhythms. Expression is Pollock's sole impetus, though being human he yearns for solace – in companionship, in celebrity, in alcohol – none of which placates his inexplicable torment for long.

Recently, an artist friend of mine bemoaned the lack of any inspirational films about artists. Indeed, most cinematic depictions of artists are bleak, depressing affairs: consider Van Gogh biopics like Vincente Minnelli's *Lust for Life* (1956) and Robert Altman's *Vincent & Theo* (1990), feminist portraits like *Camille Claudel* (1989) and *Artemisia* (1997), or downbeat contemporary fare like *Basquiat* (1996). Like so many tragic cinematic portraits of artists, *Pollock* is in the end defined by the terminal cul-de-sac of the painter's final years, aching for fresh avenues that eluded him, wallowing in the dregs of countless drinking binges (Harris beautifully captures the moment of fatal resignation, too, in the last glimpse of his face as he drives to his fate).

But as actor and director, Harris thankfully communicates the realities downplayed in other such films: the feast and famine nature of making one's living creatively; the lively communication between artists via their work; the act of creation as a restless, revelatory exploration. Harris does so with rare insight, ferocity, and skill, just as he conveys the savagery and despair that ultimately consumed Pollock. Nor does Harris short shrift the people in Pollock's orbit: Marcia Gay Harden is especially fine as Pollock's put-upon partner, Lee Krasner, and deservedly won an Academy Award for her efforts. Despite its lapses and missteps, *Pollock* is a fierce, devotional work, and one of the summer's few 'must see' offerings.

Rabid cinematic devotion – the absolute *need* to create – likewise fuels a fresh crop of fine short films by local filmmakers that recently graced the big screen en route to video. *"The Rozefire Film Festival"* debuted at the Bellows Falls Cinema on August 4th, offering a generous selection of work by local filmmakers Jake and Alex Stradling, Shandor Garrison, Chad Goyette, and David and Suzanne Groenewold.

Jake Stradling's ***JUDGMENT*** and Chad Goyette's ***NOTHING TO FEAR*** are essentially exercises in style, and as such they are slight, but a lot of fun. The former depicts a young vigilante (Macklen Makhloghi) prompted to take action against armed robbers while visiting an ice cream stand; the latter plunges its teenage protagonist (Dorien Makhloghi) into a nightmarish encounter that may or may not be real. Both are energetic, engaging potboilers, effectively raising pulses and hackles while showcasing the considerable onscreen charisma of the Makhloghi brothers. I also enjoyed the music videos on view (Jake's *One Man's Carnage*, Alex's *The Birthday Wish*, and David Groenewold's *Soul Collector*, the latter featuring local fave band Intercept), but the real surprises for me were Alex's 35 minute *Painful Grace* (2001) and Shandor Garrison's *No One's a Mystery* (2000).

PAINFUL GRACE chronicles the oddly touching accidental rendezvous between a lone wolf hitman (Dan August) and a suicidal young woman (Maiana Borsody) in a nondescript, remote roadside motel. Maintaining a rigorous focus on the criminal's perception of events (including delusional encounters with bloodied victims who visit him during his furtive lapses into sleep), director Alex builds to a potent, nicely understated climax. Even better is Shandor Garrison's ***NO ONE'S A MYSTERY***, adapted from the short story by Elizabeth Tallent, which runs less than nine minutes. In a succinct exchange of dialogue between a cheating husband (Doug Smith) and his young teenage lover (Maiana Borsody, in another brief but affecting performance), *No One's a Mystery* weaves richer, more resonant characterizations than most feature films manage in ten times the running time. For my money, this poignant gem is the pearl of the collection, and one of the best short films I've seen in years.[37]

These creative individuals need and deserve your support... and, I daresay, reward such an investment more than much of the Hollywood tripe we habitually pour our rental dollars into. Despite tight shooting schedules and almost nonexistent budgets, this eclectic collection of shorts offered more surprises and substance than most big-budget studio fare.

It isn't the promise of better things to come (though that promise is self-evident) that I find so compelling

---

[37] It is, in fact, a *perfect* short film – and one I've since utilized in the classroom as a teacher at The Center for Cartoon Studies. Kudos to Shandor Garrison, who has since completed the short films *Freebox* (2003; see *Green Mountain Cinema I*) and *Jim the Rapist* (2007).

here; it's the passion, the *heat*, the real accomplishments on view, and the genuine heights and depths these young filmmakers already reach that is so invigorating.

They do it for love – for love of cinema.[38]

August 23:

HANNIBAL (2001): Novelist Thomas Harris originally fabricated Hannibal Lecter, M.D., as a supporting character in his seminal serial killer / police procedural thriller *Red Dragon* (1981). As fictional creations sometimes do, Lecter thereafter took on a life of his own. Gorged on public interest and adulation, Lecter took root and blossomed in the mass consciousness, assuming some form of sentient existence outside that of his creator. Like Frankestein contemplating Frankenstein's monster, Harris found himself caught in the glare of his own creation, peering back at him from the world outside: from book jackets and movie posters, from the big and little screen.

In a new foreward for the most recent paperback reprint of *Red Dragon*, Harris wrote, *"I found, and find, the scrutiny of Dr. Lecter uncomfortable, intrusive, like the humming in your thoughts when they X-ray your head."* Harris also notes he had no intention of revisiting the doctor's cell: *"Years later when I started* The Si-

---

[38] This was originally written and published in two parts; I have only removed and revised the transitional opening paragraph to what was part two, the August 16th column, and deleted the mail order information for Rozfire's videocassette, which is long out of print.

lence of the Lambs, *I did not know that Dr. Lecter would return."*[39]

But return he did, with a vengeance. Indelibly gnawing his way into our collective pop culture with his leap from the page to the screen, Lecter earned Anthony Hopkins an Oscar for bringing the good doctor to cinematic life. As a novel, *Silence of the Lambs* was a bestseller (1988) and, as a film (1991), a boxoffice hit and Academy Award winner. It took Harris another decade to complete *Hannibal* (1999), which divided readers, fans, and literary critics.

Ridley Scott's film of *Hannibal* (2001) has likewise divided viewers and critics. Comparisons with director Jonathan Demme's celebrated feature adaptation of *The Silence of the Lambs* are inevitable, though unfair: *Silence* was a suspense thriller, *Hannibal* most decidedly is not. *Hannibal* the movie is as different from *Silence of the Lambs* as that Academy-Award sweeper was from *Manhunter* (1986), Michael Mann's deceptively cool, calculated film version of *Red Dragon*, in which Lecter was marvelously played by Brian Cox.[40] (PS: here's a bit of bar trivia: the only actor to appear in all three films is Frankie R. Faison, graduated from a bit part in *Manhunter* to play Barney, the asylum aid, in *Silence* and *Hannibal*.)

In the meantime, the wake of Harris' influential novels and their respective film versions has had an ines-

---

[39] *"Foreward to a Fatal Interview,"* Harris, *Red Dragon*, Dell Books, 1981/2000, pp. xi-xii.

[40] A little over a year later, director Brett Ratner and screenwriter Ted Tally's remake/re-adaptation *Red Dragon* (2002) opened theatrically (October 4, 2002). It was, and remains, the least of the 'Hannibal' film adaptations, to my mind.

timable impact. Chris Carter's durable *The X Files* and short-lived *Millennium* series owe an enormous debt to Harris' work (what is Dana Scully, if not Claris Starling in a parallel dimension?), as do countless other novels, films, and TV series which followed.[41]

Thus, the expectations attached to *Hannibal* – the novel and movie – could never be met. Harris, thankfully, wrote the novel he had to write, rather than one suited to the *vox populi* consensus. Ridley Scott made the film he wished to make, and it is, to my mind, a magnificent work (as is Harris novel), though many revile both. For my money, Scott – whose *Alien* (1979) and *Blade Runner* (1982) upped the ante for both the horror and science fiction genres in their day – has captured the uncanny rhythms, allure, beauty, audacity, and brutal ferocity of Harris' novel. Though most critics ravaged the film (reacting only to its gore quotient, which is considerable, and finding it wanting in the shadow of *Silence*), audiences enthusiastically embraced the experience, if boxoffice returns are any yardstick.

Why? How could such a catalogue of atrocities so capture our imaginations?

Make no mistake, *Hannibal* is not for the squeamish. Building upon *Silence of the Lambs*, *Se7en* (1995), and their ilk, this is one of the most graphic films (in terms of its explicit carnage; the film is sexually chaste) ever to emerge from a major Hollywood studio (two, in fact, as the film is an MGM/Universal coproduction). The final act features a grisly dining spectacle that left

---

[41] I would now argue that the entire 'forensic police procedural' genre thriving on television owes its existence to the forensic autopsy sequences of Demme's *Silence of the Lambs*, and thus Harris's seminal novel, too.

theatrical audiences giddy, groggy, or bolting for the exit, a mindboggling banquet capping an unappetizing appetizer of charnelhouse images I cannot describe in a family newspaper.

Hannibal is, after all, a horror tale, but its horrors aren't gratuitous. The nasty particulars of novel and film serve the narrative. Harris evokes an insane, utterly corrupt world populated by reprehensible beings in privileged seats of power – hideously disfigured pedophiles, predatory career opportunists, mercenary hitmen who breed flesh-eating boars. In polar opposition to these monsters, Lecter's peculiar blend of cold rationality and rigid code of honor is admirable, once his ethics are grasped. (Though a *bona fide* aesthete, he's something of a bottom feeder – eating only those people who, in his estimation, don't deserve to live.)

Lecter is the red satellite orbiting the bright star of agent Clarice Starling (played here by Julianne Moore), drawn ever closer to her. We understand and share the attraction, as Starling's stoic loyalty, decency, and integrity remain constant in the face of ruthless usury schemes to strip her of every shred of dignity – a worthy continuation of the feminist subtext initiated in *Silence of the Lambs*. Though she swims through almost incomprehensible human corruption, Agent Starling resolutely, and not without some anguish, maintains her focus, her self, and her ideals about a Bureau that increasingly stinks of bureaucracy.

The fairy tale roots of this modern 'Beauty and the Beast' tale are self-evident. Hannibal is among the most potent of our current bogeymen, a worldly contemporary twist on the cannibalistic ogres, trolls, and feral devourers of yore. In that context, Starling (as embodied by Jodie Foster in *Silence*) is Gretel. Foster's Clarice was the young woman (an FBI agent cutting her teeth) coming of age by confronting genuine monsters (Buffalo Bob, Hannibal Lecter) and surviving. Much of the power and popularity of *Silence* was derived from that novel/film's insistent thrusting of the reader/viewer into Starling's reality as she asserted herself in a dangerous world governed by male power, from its most politically insidious (her FBI superior's exclusionary use of her gender throughout) to its most maliciously primal (Buffalo Bob's flayed victims). By doing so, Harris, Demme, and Foster prompted us to vicariously feel and share Clarice's experiences with startling emotional immediacy.

Hannibal eschews the intensity of *Silence*: its tone is meditative, its orientation oddly contemplative despite the blood-and-thunder excesses of its key setpieces. That tone is the film's strength, not a liability, appropriate to its center. This is, after all, Hannibal's story, though Starling remains the central figure in his tale.

Julianne Moore, justifiably, plays Clarice Starling as a different person, a survivor emotionally stripmined by the events that followed *Silence* (a gap succinctly summarized in the new film's harrowing opening, a botched raid that echoes the Ruby Ridge and Waco debacles). The inversions of *Silence* are unsettling: wrongfully blamed for the mess, Starling is stripped her of her hard-earned FBI rank and position, and effectively imprisoned in the subterranean FBI lab (just as Lecter was entombed underground in *Silence*), incarcerated by the Machiavellian schemes of her superior, Paul Krendler (Ray Liotta). Lecter, initially in repose in Florence until stirred from his lair, moves freely, lured by the front-page news (bait) of Starling's plight – dire circumstances orchestrated by Krendler at the behest of the vengeful

Mason Verger (Gary Oldman, virtually unrecognizable but brilliant), the scarred-and-crippled sole survivor of Lecter's previous crimes, and a major collector of Lecter memorabilia. Ensnared in Verger's web, Lecter is captured, prompting Starling to break her bonds in pursuit of – what? Lecter's capture? Or his – and her own – rescue?

Hannibal was critically lambasted as a horror film, yet it is every inch of that. It is, in fact, as literate and lavish a horror film as any ever made, thanks to the skills of author Harris, screenwriter Steven Zaillian (co-credited with David Mamet, who completed on an earlier script draft), director Scott, and a sterling cast led by Anthony Hopkins (fresh from his triumphant turn in Julie Taymor's adaptation of William Shakespeare's gore-and-cannibalism peppered *Titus*, 1999). The deepest horrors and profoundly touching moments emerge from the way novel and film arouse our appetite for some consummation of the bond between Lecter and Starling – a union which Harris' novel took to its inevitable conclusion, though the film cleverly concocts another satisfactory finale (and far more populist resolution, without betraying either Lecter or Starling's characterizations).

Among the many DVD extras is another version of the film's climax (a new ending as commercially necessary as that crafted for Lewis Teague's film adaptation of Stephen King's darkest novel, *Cujo*, 1983); note, too, that the feature's disturbing coda is a shuddery extrapolation of an interlude borrowed from the novel's midpoint. But as composer Hans Zimmer says in the 'making of' documentary *Breaking the Silence* (also featured on the DVD; Zimmer's score, by the way, with a memorably perverse interpretation of *"The Blue Danube,"* is exquisite), the film is *"really a comedy love story...*

[with] *a little opera in it."* Internet film critic David Steinberg was the only writer who picked up on this fact, unapologetically detailing his great affection for "Hannibal" as *"an achingly tender, almost sappy, celebration of the purity of improbable love in a world gone mad."*[42] Believe it or not, that's true – though I warn you, *Sweet November* it's not. The comedy is pitch black, the love story – chaste and ethical, albeit awash in blood, gristle, and bone – is set amid an almost medieval morality play.

Steinberg was also the only critic to evoke the vital link between Hannibal as pop icon and the current political landscape from which he emerged. One needn't be a Jungian to recognize the *zeitgeist* at work: the Victorian era bogeyman was once a fixture of cautionary nursery rhymes and fairy tales, but today's bogeymen speak to our adult realities. As embodied by Anthony Hopkins (who coincidentally played Nixon in Oliver Stone's biopic), the cinematic Hannibal of *Silence of the Lambs* was the cultural bogeyman of the Gulf War George H. W. Bush presidency, while Hopkins' *Hannibal* incarnation coincidentally ushered in the first 100 days of George W. Bush's presidency.

Like it or not, we unconsciously find or create the bogeymen we crave, need, and deserve. Hannibal Lecter is *the* Bush era bogeyman, bookending the dynasties of father and son – embodying not the craven politicians and opportunists we are saddled with, but a vengeful being able to see through sanctimonious abuses of wealth and power, potent enough to oppose and destroy opportunists and criminals who hide behind the veils of sanctioned greed, piety, and self-righteousness.

---

[42] *Comes Naturally* #107, February 27, 2001, archived online at http://www.sexuality.org/authors/steinberg/cn107.html

Hannibal addresses our own sense of powerlessness, our collective hunger for redress, as precious few contemporary novels or films can, will, or do. Lecter acts upon the impulses Starling (and we) cannot, or will not. Lecter admires Starling's unswerving dedication to her principals, though it demands her allegiance to corrupt 'superiors' Lecter can only despise, curs unworthy of her devotion. Despite the betrayals she suffers, Starling continues to serve the laws of a 'civilized' society which Lecter perceives as a fabric of lies, which she observes out of an unmovable loyalty and truthfulness that, in the climactic scene, forces Lecter to admit – with the fateful swing of a cleaver – that she is better than he. Lecter's culinary comeuppance of Starling's most devious foe resonates not only for its gut-wrenching *Grand Guignol* spectacle, but because justice of a kind is served.

With his elegant manner, cultured intellect, glittering eyes, and ravenous jaws, the good doctor embodies a kind of relentless moral clarity and intergrity we cannot help but respond to – and that makes him the most terrifying bogeyman of all.

*(*Hannibal *is deservedly rated a very strong 'R' – you've been warned!)*[43]

---

[43] This review was the cover feature in *Video Watchdog* #81, March 2002, pp. 40-44, with an excellent additional essay *"The Disc"* by Tim Lucas (pp. 45-47). This archived version incorporates almost all of editor Tim Lucas's changes to the text, of which I heartily approved; it was the *Reformer* version that was slightly abridged.

August 30:

15 MINUTES: Back in 1988, a clutch of creative Chicago-based advertising filmmakers and stage actors pooled their meager financial resources and formidable talents to craft *Henry: Portrait of a Serial Killer*.[44] Bucking the exploitation expectations of their financiers (who were expected a mainstream horror movie), neophyte director John McNaughton and new-to-the-screen actors Michael Rooker, Tom Towles, and Tracy Arnold created such an unflinching, disturbing experience that the MPAA flatly refused to grant an 'R' rating to the film. The organization could not cite any particular cuts that would detour the dreaded 'X' rating (the ineffectual 'NC-17' rating did not exist at the time). It wasn't the violence *per se* that was considered objectionable; McNaughton's straightforward, non-sensationalistic approach eschewed the usual horror-movie excesses. The ratings board objected to the very tone (read: existence) of the film – and, though the organization denies any preferential treatment to studio fare, the fact that *Henry* was an independent (read: non-MPAA affiliated) production also counted against it. Unable to secure theatrical distribution without a rating, *Henry* was quietly shelved until a clutch of festival showings in 1991 garnered a groundswell of fierce critical support and positive audience reactions that understood the film.

One of the most unsettling sequences in the film involved Henry (Rooker) and white trash acolyte Otis (Towles) videotaping the ruthless murder of a family. The crime was shown through the lens of the camcorder, pulling back from the action to show the killers sprawled

---

[44] See *Blur, Vol. 1*, pp. 101, 105.

on a couch, watching in rapt boredom, as they played and replayed the atrocity on their VCR. The spectacle of sociopathic coach potatoes entranced by their own horrific home videos (succinctly defining the moral gulf between the two characters by the fact that Henry doesn't want to watch the tape again, while Otis does) fused brutality and banality with marrow-chilling directness. First-time viewers watching *Henry* today won't react as strongly, though, as the scene's horror has been diffused by copycat moments in subsequent, lesser films, and dulled by a generation of numbing 'reality TV' horrors beamed into our living rooms via cable or satellite with narcotic regularity. The nuances of our individual moral universes are being gauged by a ratings process of another kind: how many of us watch such programming, and how often? The answer to both questions is self-evident, given the escalation of 'reality TV' fare.

Which brings us to *15 Minutes*, a decidedly sensationalistic thriller from New Line Cinema (a subsidiary of Warner Bros.) which the MPAA had no problem slapping an 'R' rating on since it plays by the Hollywood studio rules from stem to stern. Make no mistake, though: *15 Minutes* is more violent than *Henry*, and its mayhem is all the more offensive for its sterility and meaninglessness. Unlike *Henry*, John Herzfeld's *15 Minutes* is an entertainment, albeit a cruel one, reveling in the very tabloid-TV violence it pretends to condemn.

The film is initially engaging and beguiling, fueled by the audience-friendly polish afforded by star power (Robert DeNiro, Edward Burns), crisp production values, and shallow directorial efficiency. The ease with which writer-director John Herzfeld taps into so many cultural touchstones (the titular reference to Andy Warhol's famous 1960s quote: every citizen will enjoy 15 minutes of fame in the future-that-is-now), phobias (murderous outsiders, illegal emigrants, urban crime, the power of the media), and urban myths ('snuff' movies) is invigorating. The first act is riveting, the second act packs a sucker-punch (which I won't give away here), but this by-the-numbers cops-and-serial-killers potboiler culminates in a concluding third act so contrived that even the most captivated viewer will find their suspension of disbelief tested beyond the breaking point. It's too bad, because the film is almost about something for two-thirds of its running time.

A pair of sociopaths – a Czech and a Ukrainian, Emil Slovak (Karel Roden) and movie-lover Oleg Razgul (Oleg Taktarov) – breeze through airport customs. They begin their NYC reign of terror with Emil failing to recoup stolen money reaped from a crime he took the fall for, and Oleg stealing a top-of-the-line video camera with which he gleefully records their increasingly savage behavior (rape, arson, torture, murder). The plot creaks into more traditional gear with the introduction of a reluctant survivor / witness, a fellow illegal Ukrainian emigrant (Vera Farmiga) who becomes the 'frail' (in hardboiled genre terminology) reliant on the dubious protections offered by homicide detective Eddie Flemming (DeNiro) and Arson Investigator Jordy Warsaw (Burns). Of course, DeNiro and Burns are forced into an uneasy partnership, and sparks (literally) fly as Emil and Oleg's rampage inevitably inflates into a metropolitan media circus once they begin to feed the tapes of their crimes to a ratings-craving tabloid TV journalist (Kelsey Grammar).

As the narrative succumbs to formula, the film's strident outrage at the media exploitation of murder most foul becomes glib and increasingly exploitative before collapsing under its own wheezing hypocrisy and narrative contrivances. As the overreaching DVD *"Infinifilm"* bells and whistles make abundantly clear, writer-director Herzfeld clearly believes the shrill hysterics (early in the bloodbath, Emil exclaims, *"I love America; no one is responsible for what they do"*) are reinforcing his supposed profundities. Don't be fooled; the smug moral posturing just makes the spectacle even more tiresome. *15 Minutes* doesn't hold a candle to sharper dissections of the subject (the French mockumentary *Man Bites Dog/C'est Arrivé Près de Chez Vous, 1991*; Oliver Stone's *Natural Born Killers*, 1994), it just makes such slippery cultural turf seem less dangerous with its maladroit melodramatics. That this kind of slick, vicious, amoral vacuous tripe breezes by with an 'R' while truly adult, fiercely moral explorations of dark human nature like *Henry* are reviled by MPAA moral watchdogs adds further insult to injury.

And that, dear reader, is a crime of another kind.

(Rated 'R' for nudity, violence, gore, strong adult and sexual content, drug and alcohol abuse, and language.)

SHORT CUTS (Recent & Recommended):

BLOOD: THE LAST VAMPIRE: This early Halloween-season treat packs some eye-popping visual tricks for anime and chiller fans alike. The narrative is slight – a taut take on *Blade* and *Buffy* tropes as a covert government organization sanctions a tough young (?) belle who dispatches demonic bloodsuckers with a samurai sword (or any other sharp implement in reach) – but the stylish storytelling, direction, and seamless wedding of 2D Japanese anime techniques with rendered '3D' (well, it looks three dimensional) CGI technology is marvelous. Not everyone's cup of tea, mind you, but well worth a look if you're at all curious about the continuing anime evolution... and a must-see landmark for devotees of the genre. Recommended.

BLOW DRY: Josh Hairnet – sorry, I mean Hartnett – has (outside of this year's *Pearl Harbor*) sported the most singularly ugly haircuts of all contemporary Hollywood teen actors. Here, he stars as a barber – sorry, hairdresser – reluctantly dragged into the National British Hairdressing competition with his terminally-ill estranged mother (Natasha Richardson) and resentful divorced father (Alan Rickman), who's still pissed at mom for running off with his hair model (Rachel Griffiths) on the eve of his own final entry in a prior NBH competition. There's more, but I'm simply not going to go into it. I couldn't get past my dread of Hartnett circling anyone's hair with a pair of scissors.

For those of you seeking some end-of-summer, beginning-of-schooldaze cheap laughs, the new release wall is positively choked with fool fodder that aims for the lowest common denominators and scores. Well, they score if lewd, crude, pubescent gross-out humor is your idea of a good time; all date from 2001.

TOMCATS is the worst of the bunch, with dimbulb wannabe cartoonist Jerry O'Connell hoping to clear a gambling debt via a bet that his perpetually cheating best bud Jake Busey will be wed. Misogynist 'ball and chain' 'hilarity' grates from beginning to end. Comedic highpoint: in grueling closeup, a lunching doctor bites into a nut-sized organ surgically excised from Busey's bod. I'm sorry, were you eating when you read that?

SAY IT ISN'T SO is almost as excruciating. It's a misbegotten Farrelly Brothers stable product (a long way from *There's Something About Mary*, 1998) – via a script credited to Peter Gaulke and Gerry Swallow – squeezing limp laughs out of a comedy-of-errors romantic comedy involving endless unfunny incest jokes, a sheared ear, and more mixed-up pending marriage woes involving Chris Klein (*American Pie*, 1999) and Heather Graham (*Boogie Nights*, 1997). Comedic highlight: amid mucho faked animal atrocities, a gag involving Klein's arm and a cow's – oh, that's right, you're eating, aren't you?

JOE DIRT stars and was co-written by David Spade. As with every other David Spade movie, if you like Spade, this is for you. If not, run away. This overlong 'epic' about a mullet-maned janitor (Spade) finding unexpected national celebrity and skirting true love thanks to his obsessive search for his abusive parents (almost worth the endurance test for the spectacle of Fred Ward sporting the daddy of all mullets) seemed interminable to me. But I'm old, and had already endured *Tomcats* and *Say It Isn't So*, and hence was addled beyond comprehension. Comedic highlight: an elderly dog can't get up because its privates are frozen to porch floorboards. Ah. Ha.

Dog lovers should steer way clear of ***SEE SPOT RUN***, which Warner Home Video is marketing as a *"family comedy,"* though it sets a new low for dog-dung humor. I don't know about you, but dog dung humor lost its punch for me in the third grade. Oh, I see – *family*. Third graders. I get it. It's supposed to be cute. I hate cute, but this ain't cute. Comedic highlight: you're eating, remember? Can I go home now?

September 6:

EXIT WOUNDS: Having spent the last few weeks denigrating even the noblest of upscale romantic parables (like *Chocolat*), it's impossible to justify the Neanderthal joys of Steven Seagal's inane action films – but I'll try. Seagal's vehicles (they are barely movies) function on a rudimentary 'cops & robbers' level that plugs into the male brain cortex (just a thin gray wrap around the vestigial reptilian core) with ingratiating immediacy. A former bodyguard-to-the-stars who made the leap to star stature with his debut lead in *Above the Law* (1988), Seagal has relentlessly ground out a feature a year, each fueled by his sub-Eastwood whisper and self-centered, pig-eyed determinism. Seagal's antics are punctuated with bone-breaking hand-to-hand mayhem (never more lethal than in his first outing) and breathtakingly reckless gunplay at the service of narratives distilled to almost infantile gut-level simplicity. Nothing clutters the breakneck dedication to the periodic eruption of Seagal-as-cyclone amid a concerto of human limbs snapped in directions they were never meant to bend to, loosely linked by righteous vigilante scenarios that make *Batman, Billy Jack, Dirty Harry*, and *Walking Tall* seem like models of diplomatic protocol.

Before Seagal peaked with the breakthrough success of *Under Siege* (1992, his only good film), his flicks were most entertaining for their utterly deadpan absurdities. Granted, the spectacle of Brooklyn's Finest blithely agreeing to provide Seagal a shotgun and a car in the opening moments of *Out for Justice* (1991) was risible enough, but every film had its lunatic highlight. Consider Seagal and company smuggling a militia-worthy arsenal through Jamaican customs without anyone noticing in *Marked for Death* (1990), or (my personal fave) Seagal's hilarious monologue about his dear old Italian emigrant father whose scissor-sharpening street business (?) succumbed to the influx of *"disposable scissors"* (!?!), a soliloquy that softens the heart of his estranged wife in *Out for Justice*. On the downside, the interminable, anti-climactic lecture Seagal delivered on behalf of saving the Alaskan wilderness in the coda of *On Deadly Ground* (1994) was stupefying, frightening, and funny because Seagal meant every word of it. This was his sermon on the Mount (*"What does it take to change the essence of man?"*), though he'd spent the prior 90 minutes blowing the precious Alaskan wilderness to fiery Kingdom Come battling nefarious oil barons (you hear that, George W? Seagal is *on to you*, bwah!). Having arrived at taking himself seriously as a political pundit, Seagal ceased to be narcotic fun; thankfully, he hasn't followed Jesse Ventura into office – yet.

Coming on the heels of a bum batch of fodder, Seagal's latest *Exit Wounds* (2001) – the titles are utterly interchangeable – made me curious when it clicked at the boxoffice and put Seagal back in business. Once again, ol' Pig Eyes (toting a bit more baggage under his slit lids and primordial brow, but otherwise formidable) is a renegade cop, demoted to 15th Precinct duty after his latest lone-wolf outrage. The opening volley is promising, as a fictional Vice Prez preaching anti-gun rhetoric[45] has his sorry ass rescued by Pig-Eyes in a deafening fusillade, and an amusing detour into an anger-management class wherein Seagal demolishes a school desk is heartening. There isn't a moment of pious reflection or dogmatic drivel after the Vice President's open-

---

[45] Definitely *not* Dick Cheney material.

ing speech to detract from the rollercoaster ride (well, the closing credits do rhapsodize over the proper methodology of using toilet paper, but that's neither here nor there). The film also benefits from cinematic blood transfusions from the Jet Li vehicle *Romeo Must Die* (2000), which loans its co-star DMX (the hip hop artist here playing a cool cookie cutting deals with corrupt cops on behalf of his imprisoned brother) and director Andrzej Bartkowiak to the mix. Bartkowiak thankfully abandons showstopping CGI trickery (which disrupted Jet Li's moves in *Romeo*) for more straightforward staging of the lively action sequences, and Tom Arnold lightens the load with his tabloid TV host role. In short, this is stupid fun for action fans.

There's nothing here to compare to the 'dear old pappa sharpening scissors' speech in *Out for Justice* – Seagal's glory days are behind him – but *Exit Wounds* does exactly what it sets out to do with ingratiating shamelessness and cold efficiency. If you're seeking something with half a brain in its skull, you'd best look elsewhere, but Seagal fans: rejoice. *(Rated 'R' for violence, gunplay, alcohol and drug abuse, nudity, adult and sexual situations, and strong language.)*

MEMENTO: Meanwhile, on the other end of the scale, consider writer/director Christopher Nolan's sophomore effort *Memento* (2001), as stimulating and stylish a genre effort as we've seen since Darren Aronofsky's audacious *Pi* (1998). Where Aronofsky spiked his brew with a heady blend of religion and mathematics, Nolan cuts to the chase with a primal 'film noir' set-up worthy of classics like the original *D.O.A.* (1949). A man named Leonard Shelby (Guy Pearce) is seen shooting another man point blank in the back of the head – in reverse. We are then immersed into Leonard's story – unreeling in reverse – as it unravels in staccato bursts, some shotgun-short, some extended into illusory moments of near-clarity.

You see, Leonard is unable to retain any short-term memories; acting on the 'knowledge' (forever relative) that his wife was raped and murdered and must be avenged, Leonard lurches toward his goal forever off-balance. His actions dangle on the tangled threads of half-remembered conversations, enigmatic observations scrawled on the backs of blurry photographs, and devoted study of the phrases he has tattooed onto his body for safe keeping. Nothing is what it seems. The further we plunge down the rabbit hole of Leonard's quest, the more we suspect those in Leonard's circle are derailing him with their own twisted agendas; the closer 'the truth' appears to be, the more elusive it becomes.

Writer/director Nolan vicariously prods us into a mind set disturbingly close to Leonard's own by telling his tale backwards, teasing and tantalizing us with fragmentary impressions, glimpses, and clues that edge into nerve-wracking focus as we are lead toward the ground zero of Leonard's personal apocalypse. The engagement with Leonard's universe is engrossing: felt as well as heard and seen, tactile and deceptively immediate. Directors like Nicolas Roeg (*Performance*, 1970, *Walkabout*, 1971, *Don't Look Now*, 1973, *The Man Who Fell to Earth*, 1976, *Eureka*, 1984, etc.) used to tell tales in similarly adventurous ways, working their narratives from both ends toward the center, so to speak, and thus setting off unexpected fireworks in the viewers' imagination. Nolan has plugged into a similar wellspring with fresh intensity, and the results are intoxicating.

Memento is a giddy trip, anchored by a tour-de-force central performance by Guy Pearce (*The Adventures of Priscilla, Queen of the Desert*, 1994, *L.A. Confidential*, 1997, *Ravenous*, 1999, *Rules of Engagement*, 2000) and excellent support from Joe Pantoliano (*The Matrix*, 1999, *The Sopranos* 2002 season, etc.) and Carrie-Anne Moss (*The Matrix, Chocolat*). This is the kind of movie I love. Despite its narrative thread (tenuous, but taut enough to earn the film mainstream success), this is indeed mind-altering cinema. After my first viewing, it took me over half an hour to regain my bearings, and I was hungry for a second viewing to experience it all anew with the fresh insights of the final (or should I say initial?) revelations.

Memento works admirably as a thriller, but it also dissects the very fabric and function of both memory and cinema with lucid precision. How and why do we put so much stock in these fleeting impressions of events, time, and characters fabricated by patterns of light and shadow flickering before our eyes? By pulling the rug out from under our feet time and time again as *Memento* runs its course, Christopher Nolan manages to do far more than merely entertain us. He forces us to ponder how thin the veil of perception truly is, how easily we are led astray by what we believe – and what we *want* to believe – is true, and demonstrates how destructive (and self-destructive) slavish devotion to forever-unverifiable 'truths' may prove.

Taken as either a thriller or deeper fare, *Memento* is a bracing achievement. This is one of the year's best, and not to be missed. *(Rated 'R' for violence, nudity, adult and sexual situations, strong language, adult themes.)*

September 13:

BLOW: Since he dominates all 123 minutes of screen-time, Johnny Depp fans will find plenty to savor in ***Blow***, an ambitious but shallow chronicle of the rise and fall of real-life cocaine entrepreneur George Jung. Boston born in the 1950s and driven by the determination to never want for the finer things in life, George (Depp) coasts into the countercultural 1960s bringing home the bacon dealing grass. The high times end with the death of a loved one, a bust, and jail time that indoctrinates Jung into the greener pastures of the nascent cocaine scene. Once out of prison, Jung played a key role in trafficking coke on an unprecedented scale in the late 1970s and early 1980s, but 'honor among thieves' soon leaves the wreckage of failed and betrayed friendships, family, and business relations in its wake.

This biographical cautionary tale finds Depp in fine form, portraying Jung throughout as an easy-going, likable opportunist undone by his own ambitions and appetite for quick cash and instant gratification. As such, Jung remains a poster-child of the 1980s, and the film initially paints a compelling portrait of the underbelly of Reaganomics which ironically blossomed and thrived as the *"Just Say No"* war on drugs was glibly defined and escalated. Despite references to Noriega and one grim sequence in which Jung meets notorious kingpin Pablo Escobar (Cliff Curtis), *Blow* skirts all political and social issues (save to credit Jung for the flow of cocaine at the close of the 1970s). However accurately this may reflect Jung's own tunnel vision in his own life, this blindered orientation ultimately trivializes the film. Even Oliver North's mum could enjoy this film and shake her head knowingly.

Director Ted Demme mustn't be confused with his uncle, Jonathan Demme (*Melvin and Howard*, 1980, *Something Wild*, 1986, *Silence of the Lambs*, 1991, etc.); Ted is an efficient but unexceptional filmmaker whose best work to date remains the wistful *Beautiful Girls* (1996). Simply put, he hasn't the chops to make *Blow* work. It's a toothless but highly watchable biopic, rendering its volatile subject palatable as an entertainment, which is undoubtably all the studio wanted. Given its subject, *Blow* is oddly sterile, superficial, and tame. Again, though its tone may be true to Jung's personality, the film is ultimately too even-keeled.

It's curious how little electricity sparks from such potentially incendiary material. The film never juices its own steady pace to evoke the pleasures and paranoia, the excess, the addictive 'buzz,' of the drugs that fuel its narrative, as did *Scarface* (1983), *Goodfellas* (1990), and *Boogie Nights* (1997). Though Jung is constantly plunged into life-and-death situations and lived as a fugitive much of his adult life, the film never communicates a sense of danger, either. Neither as involving or potent as its contemporary *Traffic* (2000, itself a pale shadow of its respective source material, the 1989 British TV miniseries *Traffik* [46]), *Blow* is a minor entry in its genre. One can only wonder what Oliver Stone or Martin Scorsese might have made of the same true-life scenario.

That said, Depp makes this worth a look. The supporting cast is attractive, too: Penelope Cruz in the thankless role of Jung's wife earns top billing, but Paul Reubens (Pee Wee Herman himself) leaves a greater impression as Jung's affable night life connection Derek Foreal. The strongest anti-drug propaganda, however, is

---

[46] See this volume, pp. 60-62.

conjured by Bobcat Goldthwait's fleeting role as a bartender sampling Jung's merchandise. Looking haggard, emaciated, and weary, once-hyperkinetic comedian Goldthwait comes across as a real casualty of the coke scene, looking frighteningly like the real George Jung (still behind bars and glimpsed in the final freeze frame before the credits). Even under the mangy shag wig and old-age makeup of his final scenes, Depp simply looks too good to match the chill Goldthwait's brief cameo provokes. *(Rated 'R' for adult and sexual situations, casual drug use and abuse, strong language, and violence.)*

SHORT CUTS (Recent & Recommended):

THE DISH: This offbeat comedy depicts the real-life exploits of the Australian eccentrics who monitored the only radio telescope (the titular dish) in the southern hemisphere capable of transmitting images of the historic 1969 Apollo 11 moon landing to the rest of the world. Framed as a reverie by aging scientist Cliff Buxton (Sam Neill, never more charming), *The Dish* avoids overt pratfalls for dry, understated absurdities, and as such stands as a warm, funny companion to director Rob Sitch's earlier *The Castle* (1997).[47] I quite liked it; recommended.

THE HOUSE OF MIRTH: Gillian Anderson, heretofore renowned for playing Scully on *The X-Files* (1993-2002) for nearly a decade, matures into one of our most radiant stars in this quiet, evocative adaptation of Edith Wharton's tale of a wayward socialite's ascent and de-

---

[47] See *Blur, Vol. 1*, pp. 116-117.

cline in turn-of-the-century New York City. Director Terence Davies navigates Anderson through her heroine turn as Lily Bart with assured skill and grace, savoring stillness and silence like a master chef bringing a dish to a proper boil. Undone by both her adherence and indifference to social conventions (and matters of the heart), Lily courts disaster with pride, foolishness, and abandon – and Anderson brilliantly renders every nuance of her tragic arc. Casual viewers may rate this on a level with watching paint dry, but those tuned to Wharton's voice and Davies' vision will be amply rewarded. Recommended.

PARADISE LOST 2: REVELATIONS: A compelling, frightening, and ultimately frustrating sequel to Joe Berlinger and Bruce Sinofsky's award-winning documentary *Paradise Lost: The Child Murders at Robin Hood Hills* (1996), which chronicled the arrest, trial, and conviction of three teenage misfits for the savage mutilation and murder of three preteen boys. As in the prior film, Berlinger and Sinofsky build a persuasive series of arguments that a major miscarriage of justice has taken place... and the clock is still ticking for all three convicted young men, one of whom remains on death row. Though the filmmakers were denied the privileged access to all participants the first film depended upon, this remains confrontational filmmaking of a high order. It's strong stuff indeed, emotionally and visually: the analysis of forensic photos of the murder victims is not for the weak of heart. The cultural impact of the first film cannot be overstated, as the content, tone, and even the website (which continues to provide updates on its subject) inspired *The Last Broadcast* (1998)[48] and the steamroller pop phenomenon of *The Blair Witch Project* (1999)[49] and its subsequent offshoots; Berlinger, in fact, directed *Book of Shadows: Blair Witch 2* (2001).[50] The most chilling element remains the possibility that the culprit most likely guilty for the horrific child murders is still at large, once again seen flaunting his involvement in an almost unbearably perverse, pious manner. Recommended, but approach with caution; most definitely for mature viewers only.[51]

September 20:

DRIVEN: Ever since the 1960s, when John Frankenheimer broke his rep for taut, brainy thrillers (*The Manchurian Candidate*, 1962, *Seven Days in May*, 1964) with the bloated, fatuous, but eye-drugging *Grand Prix* (1966), big-bucks racing flicks have been the pits. Think *Red Line 7000* (1965, with James Caan), *Winning* (1969, Paul Newman), *Le Mans* (1971, Steve McQueen), *Bobby Deerfield* (1977, Al Pacino), *Days of Thunder* (1990, Tom Cruise): the on-the-track action is riveting, the off-the-track banter and bathos blows like a dual exhaust. The only exceptions to this rule of the road are low-budget affairs: two sturdy biopic sleepers, *The Last American Hero* (1973, starring Jeff Bridges as Junior Johnson) and *Heart Like A Wheel* (1983, with Bonnie Bedelia as Shirley Muldowney), and Paul Bartel's *Death*

---

[48] See *Blur, Vol. 1*, pp. 136-138, 176-182.
[49] See *Blur, Vol. 1*, pp. 79-88.
[50] See *Blur, Vol. 3* , pp. 139-141.
[51] At the time of this writing, *Paradise Lost 3* is still in production.

Race 2000 (1975), the subversive sf satire which sported Sylvester Stallone's most (deliberately) hilarious performance ever. In his post-*Rocky* (1976) climb to stardom, Stallone disowned *Death Race 2000*, but he should have siphoned some fuel from that relic to rev up his vapid screenplay for his latest star vehicle, *Driven* (2001).

Yes, Stallone wrote *Driven*, but don't forget he wrote *Rocky*, too; he does (or did) know how to craft a script. Like *Rocky*, this opus focuses on competitive athletes under pressure; unlike *Rocky*, any sense of intimacy (which lent *Rocky* its heart) is drowned in overblown melodrama and – typical of this genre – the spectacle of the track. And as was the case with Frankenheimer back in 1966, director Renny Harlin (*Die Hard 2: Die Harder*, 1990, *Cliffhanger*, 1993, *The Long Kiss Goodnight*, 1996, *Deep Blue Sea*, 1999,[52] etc.) excels only when the spectacle dominates the screen. As in *Grand Prix*, the lavish budget affords an international arena (Toronto, Tokyo, Detroit) that does nothing for the turgid drama. Once the cipher characters are shoved offscreen or strapped into their vehicles, though, *Driven* lives up to its title in spades.

The tedious narrative drags whenever it's pounding pavement with the washed-out veteran pro racer (Stallone), trying to bang some sense into the up-and-coming rookie (Kip Pardue, who registered as a young long-hair football player in *Remember the Titans*) while butting heads with the scatter-shot reigning champ (Til Schweiger), demanding team proprietors (Burt Reynolds, coasting) and promoters (Robert Sean Leonard), and the embittered ex (Gina Gershon), among others.

---

[52] See *Blur, Vol. 1*, pp. 141-142, and *Blur, Vol. 2*, pp. 231-232.

Yawn. But when the pedal hits the metal and rubber burns, hold on to your popcorn.

Thanks to the latest camera technology (enhanced, natch, with cutting-edge CGI), *Driven* puts the viewer in the driver's seat, showcasing the most ruthless racing sequences in cinema history. Only then does the film come to life, fusing gasping breath, sternum-thrumming vibrations, and G-force distortions of audio and imagery with the adrenaline rush of high-speed acceleration and literally gut-wrenching mayhem of maximum impact demolition. Action fans and speed freaks won't be disappointed, and DVD addicts with amped sound systems will revel in the intoxicating track madness (unlike most home viewers, they'll be ducking the metal shrapnel ripping from speaker to surround-sound speaker). And that's all *Driven* is about, after all. Your own need for speed will determine your orientation to Stallone's latest (ahem) star vehicle. Gentlemen, start your engines... *(Rated "PG-13" for strong language and action.)*

BLOOD SIMPLE: The Coen Brothers, Ethan and Joel, cut their (and hungry audiences') eye teeth on this potent thriller set in rural Texas, where, we're immediately warned by a bit of offscreen wisdom from private dick Loren Visser (M. Emmet Walsh), *"you're on yer own."* You betcha. With *Blood Simple* (1983), the Coen Brothers redefined film noir and independent cinema for a new generation (hand in hand with David Lynch's *Blue Velvet*, three years later), and this newly restored re-release still packs surprising punch for an eighteen-year old.

A vicious triangle between desperate Abby (Frances McDormand), her lover Ray (Ray Getz), and brooding cuckolded husband Marty (Dan Hedaya) turns venomous when Marty offers ten grand to sleazy private investigator Visser (Walsh) to kill his cheating wife and her lover. That's all I can tell you, as the devil is in the details. Be warned that the Coens turn the thumbscrews to excruciating extremes, edging into real nightmare turf before the harrowing final act.

The star turn belongs to character actor M. Emmet Walsh, vet of over one hundred films, who steals the show in his butterball suit and tarnished VW beetle, forever orbited by a fly or two. Walsh embodies the worst instincts of a genre stereotype as venerable as Visser's Texan drawl; his marvelous performance provides the film's richest, blackest vein of humor. When he chortles, *"you give me a call whenever you want to cut off my head – I can always crawl around without it,"* you believe he could – and would.

True to the Coens subsequent films, the sweaty cast of characters are none too bright, hence the title, Texan slang for those sorry souls driven to stupid actions by blood (of which there is an abundance). This lends the proceedings a believability and gravity few films of its kind muster. In fact, all the characters essentially lose their heads, so to speak, and crawl around in the dark without a lick of sense: blood simple, indeed. Among the many pleasures of revisiting this gem is the revelation that none of the characters could, in a million years, piece together what actually transpires. The Coens see to it that only the audience is privileged with enough information to grasp the chain of events, and the inevitable descent into darkness.

The term 'restoration' for this 'Director's Cut' is deceptive, and critics reviewing the theatrical re-release reported cuts that simply weren't made. The new prints are gorgeous, but the running times are virtually identical. The Coens cut mere seconds, including two very brief bits of dialogue from the bartender Maurice (Samm-Art Williams): an early, momentary exchange with a barfly from Lubbock over the jukebox (*"What night is this? Friday night is Yankee night..."*) was shorn, along with a single sustained shot in the penultimate act between Abby and Maurice (its key dialogue is now dubbed over the remnants of the shot to sustain the narrative). A few frames of Marty groping Abby as he drags her out of Ray's apartment were also cut, or the shot was reframed to eliminate that detail. Visually and narratively, the film hasn't otherwise been tampered with one iota. It just looks – and sounds – even better.

In short, the major difference between the original *Blood Simple* and this 'new' version is a revised soundtrack, remixed for Dolby to beef up (and at times subdue) the sound and supplant two 1983 musical arrangements by Jim Roberge with new material. Roberge's lively version of *"I'm A Believer"* (an ironic anthem which figured in three key scenes, including the bracing final shot and credits roll) is replaced by The Four Tops standard *"It's the Same Old Song,"* sadly to lesser effect; Roberge's bouncy instrumental *"Nada Mucho"* (heard on the radio during the grueling roadside scene that launches the film's most horrific stretch, later echoed in Abby's apartment behind choice words betwixt the estranged lovers) is gone, making way for the Xavier Cugat chestnut *"The Lady in Red."* I'd have preferred a proper restoration of the original musical elements – *"I'm A Believer"* worked beautifully, adding one last fillip of black comedy to the final shot – but legal issues may have necessitated the changes. Gone, too, is the country classic *"He'll Have to Go,"* though its replacement (Patsy Cline's *"Sweet Dreams"*) works just fine in its place (hitting its first beat after Cline's sustained opening croon just as the camera settles back to the bar after drifting over an unconscious drunk).

Whether it's your first time around or a revisit, *Blood Simple* is well worth a look. Savored with the hindsight of the unique films the Coen Brothers have since graced us with, *Blood Simple* is an eloquent reminder of what the boys were capable of straight out of the starting gate. It's weathered the test of time, still standing head and Stetson above most of today's so-called 'thrillers' that don't thrill (and by and large suck like a bucket of ticks). Highest recommendation – but let the squeamish beware. *(Rated "R" for strong language, adult and sexual content, violence, and casual alcohol use and abuse.)*

September 27:

ALONG CAME A SPIDER: There's not much to say about this slick, efficient, empty adaptation of James Patterson's first novel featuring forensic psychologist Dr. Alex Cross (Morgan Freeman). Previews gave away too many plot points; I won't commit the same crime here (what few narrative surprises the film has it desperately needs). Suffice to say, after one of the most jarring opening sequences in recent memory, Cross is reluctantly drawn into a case involving a Senator's kidnapped daughter (Mika Boorem). That's all you'll get out of me, save to note that *Along Came A Spider* is, in fact, the prequel to *Kiss the Girls* (1997), which also starred Freeman as Cross. Freeman was the primary virtue of that mediocre gothic serial killer thriller, and he's the only reason to spend time with *Along Came a Spider*.

Freeman is one of our finest living American actors, lending a galvanizing fusion of heart, intelligence, and world-weary wisdom to the weakest of his films... and this, sad to say, is among the least of those. It's not a complete disaster, mind you: the opener is a doozy, and director Lee Tamahori (*Once Were Warriors*, 1994, *Mulholland Falls*, 1996, *The Edge*, 1997 – all better films by far) keeps the pace brisk enough to divert one from the widening plot holes. There's a story point in the first act that some viewers may miss completely: sans a certain amount of computer savvy, old-timers won't have a clue how Cross makes one huge deductive leap. You may need a teenager around to explain it to you, so don't be ashamed to ask. In its closing moments, the film's increasingly sloppy storytelling relies on the hoariest of impossible computer tricks (*all* the facts, at your fingertips, in mere seconds!) to justify its creaky *deus ex machina* finale. Freeman deserves better, and so do you. *(Rated "R" for strong language, violence.)*

SPY KIDS: Here's a lively high-octane fantasy for 'tweeners – the latest Hollywood demographic group in need of fleecing – from writer/director/editor Robert Rodriguez (*El Mariachi*, 1992, *Desperado*, 1995, *From Dusk to Dawn*, 1996), who is determined not to fleece the audience, but entertain, and he does so handsomely. *Spy Kids* was proclaimed *"the* 'Chitty Chitty Bang Bang' *for 2000"* by its star Antonio Banderas, but it's better than that. *Chitty Chitty Bang Bang* (1968) was a bloated, overlong musical monstrosity; *Spy Kids* is sassy, funny, and it moves like a rollercoaster ride while remaining unapologetically silly. It's an action movie for younger viewers, sans the mean-spirited mayhem of the 'adult' (more often adolescent) model, and a sly parody of 1960s spy movies, gleefully pirating plot points from creaky such mid-'60s Bond wanna-bes like *In Like Flint* (1967) and the Vincent Price *Dr. Goldfoot* films (1965/66, both featuring female robots created to seduce and destroy) and sharper TV fare like *The Man From U.N.C.L.E.* (1964-68), *The Avengers* (1961-69), and *Get Smart* (1965-70).

The title is a triple entendre, referring to Carmen (Alexa Vega) and Juni (Daryl Sabara), offspring (hence, 'spy kids') of married retired spies Gregorio and Ingrid Cortez (Antonio Banderas and Carla Gugino in infectious high spirits). Carmen and Juni soon become 'spy kids' themselves, forced into the espionage game when their parents are kidnapped by the scheming egocentric Fabulous Fegan Floop (Alan Cummings) and resident renegade evil genius Alexander Minion (Tony Shalhoub), who have created a brood of malicious robot children which they call Spy Kids. Got that? But wait, there's more, including Minion's minions, the Thumb Thumbs (humanoid henchmen composed entirely of thumbs), Floop's Flooglies (cartoonish co-stars of Floop's kid show which are actually imprisoned, mutated secret agents), and cameos from George Clooney, Cheech Marin, Mike Judge (creator of *Beavis and Butthead*, 1992-97, *King of the Hill*, 1997-present, etc.), and Richard Linklater (director of *Slackers*, 1991, *Dazed and Confused*, 1993, etc.). It's also great to see grizzled character actor Danny Trejo in a sympathetic role for a change (as Gregorio's estranged brother).

Emulating the streamlined pacing and eye-popping special effects of 1990s action thrillers, Rodriguez lovingly plunders the freakish invention and excess of Hollywood's classic children fantasy films, from *The Blue Bird* (filmed at least five times between 1910-1976) and *The Wizard of Oz* (1939) to *The 5000 Fingers of Dr. T* (1953) and *Willy Wonka and the Chocolate Factory* (1971). The inspired creature creations (by the maestros at KNB) are vivid and scary without being ghoulish, and the colorful set, costume, and effects designs pack a pleasing storybook punch while adhering to the plastic action genre archetypes the film delightfully inflates and deflates at every turn. All in all, *Spy Kids* is a lot of fun – and exactly the kind of film its target audience might take to heart the same way prior generations adopted the Wizard, Willy Wonka, and the Goonies. *(Rated "PG" for mild violence.)*

STARTUP.COM: This insightful, gripping, ultimately devastating documentary chronicles the birth, rise, and fall of one of the 'dot com' companies behind the stock market collapse that dragged the national economy down with it. Under the producer wing of vet documentarian D. A. Pennebaker, directors Jehane Noujaim and Chris Hegedus lucked into an insider's view of a firm co-founded by Amherst, New Hampshire high school graduates Kaleil Isaza Tuzman and Tom Herman. Friends since age fifteen, Tuzman and Herman were in their late twenties when they launched (with a third partner) 'govworks.com,' an internet business designed to facilitate on-line interaction between individuals and local government (licensing, tickets, town meetings, etc.). *"Life, Liberty, and the Pursuit of More Efficient Government"* was their motto, and Tuzman and Herman's struggles to secure the necessary capital and manpower to bring their dream to fruition is immediately engaging.

Tuzman and Herman are soon butting heads over contradictory strategies and focus. Fifteen minutes of screen time later, having raised over $15 million to finance their venture (at that point, already valued at $50 million), they've grown from eight to seventy employees, and have ruthlessly bought out their third partner. On his way out the door, the 'third wheel' founder says, *"One of the saddest things about business... is when you watch ideas grow beyond what you can do for them,"* a succinct insight into all that follows. Soon, Tuzman is earning cover spots on key business zines while serving with President Clinton on a government committee (and, in a flight of hubris, offering a job to the former President!), jockeying to usurp his life-long buddy for 'the good of the company,' while stiff competition, corporate espionage, and the collapse of the Wall Street bubble take their cumulative toll.

The events that unreel onscreen (filmed May, 1999 to December, 2000) offer a sobering portrait of the kind of ambitious entrepreneurs that launched – and sank – a thousand flagships in the brave new world of online commerce. *Startup.com* is a terrific film, yielding surprising drama as the bond between Tuzman and Herman unravels, even as their fondest dreams are realized beyond their wildest expectations. The filmmakers dissect the human cost of the closed-door follies with engaging intimacy. The growth and demise of a partnership through the rigors of boom, bust, and seemingly inevitable acquisition by a multinational corporation is vividly conveyed – prompting one to wonder, is this a snapshot of the Great American Dream of the 1990s, or the all-too-typical life of human plankton in the current global corporate ocean our government has willfully nurtured? This is necessary viewing for Ben & Jerry aficionados, and the first 21st Century classic of its overlooked genre (see Rod Serling's *Patterns*, 1956; Michael Mann's *The Insider*, 1999; and *The Pirates of Silicon*

Valley, 1999[53]). Highly recommended! *(Ridiculously rated "R" for strong language; what hooey.)*

SHORT CUTS (Recent & Recommended):

DRAINIAC: For a sampler of what another New Hampshire entrepreneur – Derry, NH filmmaker Brett Piper – is capable of, check out this cheapjack exploitation gem. *Drainiac* (an invisible water sprite) infects the plumbing of an understandably abandoned house, feeding on stray derelicts until nasty stepfather (Steven Bornstein) exiles stepdaughter Julie (Georgia Hatzis) there for an afternoon. Clean-up and renovations take a back seat to vile manifestations of the titular spook, which slithers in and out of drains, toilets, and burst pipes reducing the supporting cast to Slurpies before a scabby exorcist (Phip Barbour) comes to the rescue. Brett Piper has been grinding out his distinctive brand of direct-to-video schlock for twenty years, meshing modest ambitions, amateur performances, and splashy nudity and gore with always-inventive stop-motion animation effects. Piper made the prehistoric mini-epics *Nymphoid Barbarian in Dinosaur Hell* (1990) and *Dinosaur Babes* (1996), the beach-monster flick *They Bite* (1993), and this, his latest, which offers more stupid fun than you'd imagine possible on a dime-store budget. It's ideal Halloween fodder. *(Unrated, but would most likely earn an "R" for nudity, language, and violence.)*

A KNIGHT'S TALE: Another guilty pleasure is this teen flick disguised as a medieval adventure. It's essentially *"Wart's Progress"* (brush up on your Arthurian

---

[53] See *Blur, Vol. 1*, pp. 141-142, and *Blur, Vol. 2*, pp. 231-232.

legends or watch Disney's 1963 *The Sword in the Stone* one more time): tousled-haired, square-jawed squire William (Heath Ledger) dons the armor of his fallen master and works his way up the tournament circuit pretending to nobility above his station and knocking tincan adversaries off their saddles. The cast is winning, the tone uneven: the film never finds its footing between *Prince Valiant* high romance and adventure, and *Monty Python and the Holy Grail* grunge, gore, and hilarity – and never cares to, anyway. Verily, the wise-ass (aka 'hip') dialogue, attitude, and jarring juxtaposition of contemporary music (Queen's *"We Will Rock You"* anachronistically accompanies the jousting events, just like TV sports) will either win you over or drive you out of the room. Safe to say, the kids would just as soon you did leave the room, anyway, leaving them to savor the spectacle of violence, valor, and hunky Heath Ledger without your damned grousing.

Note: Due to the necessity of removing a trailer for *Spider-Man* (which featured imagery of the World Trade Center), the video release of *A Knight's Tale* was delayed until *tomorrow*, September 28th. However, the DVD (which never sported the problematic trailer) streeted Tuesday, Sept. 25th. *(Rated "PG-13" for language, adult situations and nudity, and knightly mayhem.)*

October 10: Visionary VT Vet Filmmaker Walter Ungerer Creates New Worlds

The fall colors are alluring enough to prompt a drive up the thruway to Northern Vermont, but there's a few marvelous interior visions that might sweeten the pot for the more adventurous of you. If you're tired of the drivel pouring out of Hollywood and believe, as I do, that cinema and video are viable art forms deserving of richer exploration than afforded by most commercial, corporate, and narrative venues, you might find the films of Walter Ungerer well worth the trip.

This Tuesday, October 16th, at 7 PM, a presentation of Walter Ungerer's recent digital film video creations will grace the screen of the Alumni Auditorium of Champlain College in Burlington. Walter Ungerer is among the Green Mountain State's most valuable artistic treasures, and this presentation offers a rare opportunity to savor not only Ungerer's imaginative short films, but also a chance to talk with the filmmaker himself. Ungerer is a warm, soft-spoken man, but he's an eloquent advocate of the arts and his own work, and his unyielding devotion to his art, path, and vision is nothing less than inspiring. Yes, it's a bit of a drive, but I urge those of you who might have missed Ungerer's local appearance this spring (at the Brattleboro Museum & Art Center on June 7th) to make the effort – this is a rare opportunity to savor a variety of intensely personal video works Ungerer has completed over the past decade.

Walter Ungerer is one of the pioneers of regional filmmaking, having stayed stubbornly in tune with his private muse for almost four decades in the face of changing times and venues in a marketplace that remains hostile to the idiosyncratic features, short films, and videos Ungerer has devoted his life to.

His earliest short efforts of the 1960s were overtly surreal works, culminated in the quartet of *Oobieland* films (1969-74). The first two *Oobieland* films were completed while Ungerer still lived in New York, growing into a four-film 'universe.' The first two entries layered imagery and sound impressionistically before transmuting, with Ungerer's move to Vermont, into the more narrative, dreamlike live-action shorts that concluded the foursome.

The domestic tensions of the Vietnam War era informed Ungerer's first feature, *Keeping Things Whole* (1972), opening the door to more ambitious work (I have yet to see this feature, though Walter promises me I'll soon have an opportunity to do so).

With *The Animal* (1976) and *The House Without Steps* (1978), Ungerer refined his cinematic vision using the Vermont landscape as his stage. *The Animal* is my personal favorite of Ungerer's features, set in a blinding winterscape in which the emotional distance between a strained husband and wife relationship blurs into a waking nightmare in which the wife mysteriously disappears... or does she? Ever embracing the rich ambiguity mainstream filmmakers and audiences abhor, Ungerer weaves an enigmatic dream realm which seems anchored in our day-to-day reality, though it is populated by spectral figures in the snow (a pair of children only the wife can see or interact with, the tracks of the titular 'animal' that is never found) and punctuated by mysterious events that defy rational analysis. *The Animal* is, essentially, a slice of New England gothic stripped of its genre trappings, distilled to its unnerving essence. Alas, this masterpiece is already a 'lost' film: its negative is lost forever, and only two worn 16mm prints and a murky video transfer remain.

The House Without Steps is Ungerer's most satisfying traditional narrative work, a somewhat caustic drama in which a single woman new to a small Northern Vermont village is gradually forced out of the community by the petty frustrations and desires of its citizenry. Ungerer chronicles the decaying orbit of those around her, unveiling the relentless effect the web of suspicions and lies have upon the blameless outsider seeking a foothold. Ungerer makes it clear she has done nothing to provoke the situation, save exist; since she is never privy to the gossip and innuendoes, the erosion is invisible to her, but its effects are inevitably felt. *The House Without Steps* offered ample proof of Ungerer's matured vision, which he further refined with the more introspective and challenging tenor, tone, and content of his semi-autobiographical *The Winter There Was Very Little Snow* (1982) and *Leaving the Harbor* (1992), his final feature which took a full decade to complete.

Much of the difficulties Ungerer struggled through to complete *Leaving the Harbor* were due to financial constraints: federal and state government funding of the arts was drying up, and Ungerer was forced to seek completion funds elsewhere. In due time, the reality of the situation forced Ungerer to redirect his creative energies completely, abandoning expensive features and film itself to embrace the increasingly accessible (and much more affordable) video and computer technologies.

While working and teaching as a visiting artist at Syracuse University, Ungerer created a six-screen video installation entitled *The Syracuse Tapes* (aka *6X6*, 1993), a portion of which he showed at his Brattleboro Museum presentation back in June. Soon after, he taught himself the necessary skills to create, animate, and manipulate imagery via computer graphics.

This necessary reorientation of Ungerer efforts eventually opened imaginative new vistas to the artist, and it is this new body of work that the Champlain College event showcases. The earliest of these new works were elegant, essentially playful animated shorts, including *Birds - 2/93* (1993), *A Warm Day Comes After a Cold Winter* (1994), and a collaborative effort with his daughter featuring a very odd menagerie of creatures shambling across the screen.

Upon this unassuming bedrock, Ungerer built a denser, more meditative series of short films; these comprise the core of Tuesday night's presentation. *Relatives in X, Y, and Z* (1996) is an eerie, evocative, oddly moving tableau of imagery melding old family photographs and live-action to potent effect; in its own way, the film echoes and extrapolates upon the faded old photos glimpsed on the walls of the possibly haunted house of *The Animal* twenty years earlier.

Ungerer's *Kingsbury Beach* (1999) carries the allure of mediated, manipulated photographic imagery further, while the most recent of Ungerer's works breaks fresh ground. Already screened in three variations, *Untitled*, *Untitled 2*, and *Untitled 2.1* (all 2001), this latest video work defies description altogether: it is, in its way, a primal mediation on the act of seeing itself. Again, its imagery reflects Ungerer's earlier work: a passage composed of streaking car headlights shimmering in the night recalls the mesmerizing opening of *The Winter There Was Very Little Snow*, as headlights from a distant icy road illuminate the brittle frost patterns laced upon a window pane. Attentive Brattleboro audiences were lucky enough to see all three versions of this new work. It's possible Ungerer may present a fresh variation (or a newer work altogether!) this week in Burlington.

This special presentation of Ungerer's most recent creations concludes a nine-stop traveling exhibition that was sponsored in part by the Vermont Arts Endowment and The Vermont Community Foundation. Though Ungerer's work is definitely not everyone's cup of tea, I highly recommend this event to those of you who love cinema, and have a strong interest in Vermont film and filmmakers.

October 17, 25: Pumpkin Pix for Kids, Seasonal Fears for Adults [54]

Given the tenor of the times, it might seem distasteful to many to invite the usual Halloween horrors into the household, but I hasten to point out that horror films have always served their function during desperate times.

Since the atrocities of September 11th and subsequent events, chillers like *Jeepers Creepers* (which offers a modern spin on E.T.A. Hoffman's 1817 tale *"The Sandman"*) and John Dahl's nail-biter *Joy Ride* (which reduced two teenagers to tears at the screening I attended here in Brattleboro last weekend) continue to click at the boxoffice. Adult critics deride both films (I, however, quite liked them both, for very different reasons), while teenagers flock to see them.

Why? Isn't there enough fear in our day-to-day world?

In traumatic times, measured doses of vicarious, imaginary terror has its virtues. At a time when we, as a country, are scouring for terrorists in every corner, when fear of flying has taken on new, more unnerving meaning, and when opening the morning mail understandably

---

[54] Note: These final two *Video Views* columns were cobbled together at the *Reformer A&E* section editor Jon Potter's request; though we'd already amicably decided to terminate the column, Jon wanted me to offer something for the Halloween season, and I complied with this two-parter, primarily comprised of slightly revised previously-published material.

prompts cold sweats, there are undeniable creature comforts to be found in movies designed to tease, tickle, or tangle our nerves. Like the fairy tales and boogeymen they emerge from, they mirror our most xenophobic dread, localize a multitude of nameless horrors, and give form to our fears. At their silliest, they allow us to briefly laugh at their contrived scares; at their most sublime, they tap into our most primal selves and coax forth genuine frissons; at their most taboo-breaking ruthlessness, they show the unshowable and speak the unspeakable.

The first 'boom' period of American horror films blossomed in the depths of the Depression, yielding venerable classics like Tod Browning's *Dracula* (1930) Karl Freund's *The Mummy* (1932), *King Kong* (1933) and James Whale's still-marvelous brood, *Frankenstein* (1931), *Bride of Frankenstein* (1935), *The Old Dark House* (1932) and *The Invisible Man* (1933). On the eve of World War 2, dear old Boris Karloff donned the Frankenstein Monster makeup again for *Son of Frankenstein* (1939). In the wake of Pearl Harbor, war-era tensions were eased by a torrent of Universal monsters (including the quartet of Kharis the Mummy films, 1940-44), and Val Lewton's exquisite, suggestive chillers (*The Cat People*, 1942, etc.). In the 1950s, B-movies addressed a new bevy of nuclear fears guised as a radiation-spawned menagerie of mutant monsters (*The Beast From 20,000 Fathoms*, 1953, *Them!*, 1954. etc.), joined by McCarthy era and Cold War invaders capable of leveling national capitols (*The War of the Worlds*, 1953, *Earth vs. The Flying Saucers*, 1956) or quietly supplanting the residents of a sleepy California town with cold-blooded, emotionless simulcrums (*Invasion of the Body Snatchers*, 1956). As adult dread of juvenile crime and delinquency soared, *I Was a Teenage Werewolf* (1957) told kids the truth they already knew: the adults didn't understand that the authorities (in this case, a psychiatrist who hypnotizes teen Michael Landon into primordial savagery) cloaked their own insidious brand of evil, and were definitely *not* to be trusted.

Though we may look back fondly at these horrors which now – in the wake of the blasphemies of *The Exorcist* (1973) and Clive Barker, the malice of Leatherface, Jason, Michael Myers, and Freddy – seem oddly comforting, make no mistake: contemporary audiences of the original *Frankenstein* (1931) indeed trembled, screamed, and even fainted in the aisles. One generation's boogeyman is the next generation's pop icon. And so it goes, decade after decade, as each generation's screen monsters simultaneously embody, popularize, and/or trivialize their own respective fears: an ecology of cultural projection.

Forgive me, then, as I indulge in a sort of *"Viewer's Guide to Halloween Horrors"* for the autumn season. I'll kick this overview off with a list I curried from my own children last year to help hapless parents who aren't sure what videos constitute 'safe' Halloween season viewing for the younger, most impressionable set. Given the dearth of family-friendly titles in this (and last) year's crop of horror videos, I asked my own offspring, Maia Rose and Daniel, to put together their own list of 'suitable-for-all-ages' family-friendly Halloween movies they'd recommend.[55]

---

[55] Maia and Daniel's Halloween best-of list was already reprinted in *Blur, Vol. 2*, pp. 239-241; for space reasons, I've elected not to reprint it here. Due to minor revisions, and the fact that it was the final column, I have decided to include my list.

Here's my 'best of' list for grownups eager to indulge in some Halloween horrors. With the notable exception of *The Bride of Frankenstein*, *none* of these are for the timid or squeamish. I've savored the genre for most of my forty-six years, and could cook up a different list tomorrow – but today, here's my current select list:

* Top 1, 2, and 3 slots may forever belong to George Romero's ***Night of the Living Dead*** (1968), ***Dawn of the Dead*** (1977), and ***Day of the Dead*** (1985); the ultimate apocalyptic American horror movies, one for each decade since the '60s. At his peak (which these certainly represent), Romero was one of our finest storytellers.

* James Whale's ***The Bride of Frankenstein*** (1935): I love all the classic 1930s horrors, but this and ***King Kong*** (1933, which also earned honors on Maia and Danny's list) are the jewels of the crown. Frightening, funny, fierce, heartfelt, and beautiful, this is one of the greatest films ever made, period.

* Georges Franju's ***Eyes Without a Face*** (***Les Yeux Sans Visage***, 1958): Finally available in its definitive form thanks to Kino Video, this chilling masterpiece modernized the French Grand Guignol tradition with spare elegance and often breathtaking poetry and horror.

* Mario Bava's ***Black Sunday*** (***La Maschera del Demonio***, 1961): A baroque black-and-white Gothic arabesque atmospherically photographed around the porcelain (and punctured) features of '60s pop icon Barbara Steele. This was the first horror movie to truly terrify me; I love it like no other.

* Ken Russell's ***The Devils*** (1971): A lethal merger of Church and State conspired to bring down the walls of the fortified French village of Loudon via a sanctioned

witchhunt targeting Father Grandier (Oliver Reed in his finest role). A delirious adaptation of the Aldous Huxley tract, still impossible to see in this country in its original uncut form.

* David Cronenberg's ***The Brood*** (1980): Cronenberg crawls under my skin like no other filmmaker. In a perverse twist on (and bitter indictment of) recovered memory and 'inner child' therapy, *"Psychoplasmics"* urges its survivor patients to externalize their internal rage, culminating in high tragedy and a startling climactic revelation. A harrowing portrait of a family ravaged by the cruel legacy of child abuse.

* Nicolas Roeg's ***Don't Look Now*** (1973): Roeg's best films do not merely unreel, they explode and implode within the mind. Drawn from Daphne du Maurier's short story, this elliptical, adult psychic thriller never fails to mesmerize, terrify, and move me.

* Tobe Hooper's ***The Texas Chainsaw Massacre*** (1974): On first viewing, the most relentless and nightmarish of contemporary horror films. On subsequent viewings, a brilliantly-crafted pitch-black comedy, too (*"Look what your brother did to the door!"*).

* David Lynch's ***Eraserhead*** (1976): This one-of-a-kind feature edges from an oppressive urban dreamscape into one of the most tactile domestic horrorshows ever committed to film. Sexual and parental fears are made flesh; the Lady in the Radiator is disturbing, but, oh, that baby!

* Mario Bava's ***Bay of Blood*** (***Reazione a Catena***, 1972, aka ***Last House, Pt. II***, ***Twitch of the Death Nerve***, etc.): The seminal 'body count' movie. Ravishing Bava cinematography, an ever-escalating procession of truly horrific murders (establishing the template for the entire *Friday the 13th* series) to gain an inheritance, and a hilarious coda.

* Lars Von Triers' **The Kingdom I** and **II** (Riget I and II, 1994, 1997): The original 1960s versions of *The Haunting* and *Carnival of Souls*, along with *Lady in White* (1987), *were* my all-time fave ghost movies – until the Dogma 95 enfant terrible usurped them all with his pair of five-hour miniseries set in a haunted hospital. That's almost ten hours of state-of-the-art horror, made for Danish TV but scarier than anything ever broadcast stateside. This literally sent shivers up my spine; highly recommended!

Happy Halloween, one and all!

Thus ended the *Video Views* column.

May - July, 2002: VSDA FILMMAKERS OF TO-MORROW reviews

Note: These were written for internal use, reviewing the submissions for July 2002 VSDA (Video Software Dealers Association) Trade Show event, a combined marketplace/panel. As was and remains my habit, I wrote these up as suitable-for-publication reviews; indeed, a few of them were ultimately submitted for publication to magazines and fanzines after the fact. Note that what I've chosen to archive here are the original drafts, including the concluding market/retailer oriented assessments of the films themselves, italicized in brackets.

BOOM: THE SOUND OF EVICTION (2001/2; Dir/Edi: Francine Cavanaugh, A. Mark Liiv, Adams Wood; 96 min.): Excellent documentary chronicles the 'dot.com'-fueled gentrification of San Francisco barrios and communities that threatened (and, in many cases, tragically displaced) thousands of middle and low-income families and individuals prior to the dramatic Millennial dot.com bust. As the tale unfolds, it becomes clear that this is a microcosm of much larger forces at work, the tale of much more than one city. As one activist puts it, *"We have lots of people and no money, while they* [those behind the gentrification projects] *have lots of money and just a handful of people... all the people that money can buy."* As the consolidation of national wealth continues to concentrate into the hands of a few (as noted at one point, as of 1999 73% of the national wealth now lies with only 10% of the population), provoking more joblessness, displacement, and homelessness, this case study will only become more relevant and painfully familiar.

The filmmakers successfully build empathy with the diverse people involved in the struggle at hand – housewives, families, senior citizens, activists, artists, communities – without losing 'the big picture' – social, economic, and political; city, nation, and world – relevant to their subject. That they do so with such focus, energy, and surprising flashes of humor and spirit is extraordinary.

By ingeniously framing the contemporary footage with snippets of a 1950s travelogue on San Francisco (without belaboring the conceit), the filmmakers offer a broader context for their subject, and cumulatively make key points with succinct visual economy. For instance, the comparison of the internet 'gold rush' with the 19th Century Gold Rush (and the vital role technology played in allowing high-echelon parties to profiteer from both events without suffering the losses less affluent investors endured) is driven home by a quick crosscut between a telegraph key being struck and a computer mouse being clicked.

This is canny documentary filmmaking of the highest order, a strong companion to Nora Jacobson's *Delivered Vacant* (1993) on the one hand and last year's *Startup.com* on the other. *Important:* Don't shut off the tape as the credits begin, as vital follow up information concerning the city sites central to the crisis Boom dissects unreels between the credits crawl. This is a fine piece of work; Recommended!

[Note, however, that this is hardly a strong commercial proposition in the rental video market. While Boom is a top-drawer accomplishment, it lacks the marketable studio clout or elements of successful rental docs like Roger and Me, The Atomic Cafe, The Thin Blue Line, and Fast, Cheap and Out of Control, *or even* Star-

tup.com. *However, the growing interest in issues such as those* Boom *analyses and the ongoing effects of similar gentrification in other US cities and towns make this an invaluable and timely addition to any video library. Whatever the market issues, the high quality of the film alone ensures that I would argue for the inclusion of* Boom *in the presentation in July.]*

THE CHAMPAGNE CLUB (2002; Dir/Scr: Joao Machado): Michael Naismith once sang about *"running from the Grand Ennui,"* but this handsomely mounted threnody plunges into the Grand Canyon of ennui. Direction, photography, art direction, music, and performances are fine and perfectly tuned with this upscale production's nihilistic descent into a self-made hell. It's a harrowing, graphic *Leaving Las Vegas* for the elite urban gallery set.

Joao Machado's debut feature bottles up a quartet of L.A.'s young art-scene nouveau rich in a remote tropical estate and lets them fester. Initially drawn together by their shared discomfort over the *"pendulum swing between art and commerce"* in which they owe their wealth & privilege to exploitation rather than creation, in due course (or, should I say, multiple courses, each more vile than the last) they destroy all the art in sight and willingly slide from boredom, narcissism, alienation and despair to self-degradation, self-mutilation, madness, coprophilia, cannibalism, and beyond.

When all is said and done (and eaten), this is gross fare, but there's no denying Machado chronicles ground-zero emotional auto-cannibalism with exquisite clarity. He also boasts impeccable credentials, both personal (the film is dedicated to his father, painter Juarez Machado, and mother, "consecrated grand culinary chef" Eliane

Carvalho) and cinematic. Machado brazenly plunders thematics, dramaturgy, and specifics from a stellar pantheon of art-(charnel)house horrors: Luis Bunuel's *The Exterminating Angel*, Marco Ferreri's *La Grand Bouffe*, Pasolini's *Salo*, and Peter Greenaway's *The Cook, The Thief, His Wife and Her Lover*, amid resonant imagery echoing Kubrick's *The Shining* (Tim's hallway visions of butchering his companions), Argento's *Suspiria* (the final closeup of Connie in a pool of blood spreading on a decoratively tiled floor), the anarchic Brazilian master work *Macunaima* (the swimming pool 'soup'), and key works by painters like Rene Magritte and others.

Machado orchestrates this tapestry without compromising the integrity of his own vision; indeed, though he borrows much and acknowledges all his debts along the way, the potent framing device – opening and closing with perfect symmetry – succinctly anchors his conceits and keeps the film from becoming merely derivative navel-gazing. That much of it is risible (nude Bruce eating and humping his man-sized portion of mashed potatoes) allows one to keep watching, even while the gorge rises. Machado intends to provoke, disgust, and outrage, but amid the current art house wave of explicit grue and sex (dominated by French imports like *Baise Moi, See the Sea, Fat Girl* and *Trouble Every Day* peppered with more domestic fare like *Titus* and *American Psycho*), *The Champagne Club* seems tame by comparison. It's nevertheless disturbing, an engaging first film; Machado is a filmmaker well worth following, a talent to watch.

[As with all the related import titles named above, 'Joe & Jill Citizen' renters will no doubt consider The Champagne Club*'s wallow in 'poor little rich kids' degradation and despair much ado about nothing, while*

gorehounds and exploitation buffs won't wade through the aristocratic angst to get to the grue. But adventurous cult, 'Metro', and art house viewers will seek this one out; buzz will build, and eye-catching packaging and promo could make this a profitable sleeper.] [56]

THE DOGHOUSE (2002; Scr/Dir: Steven Kane; 93 min.): *"There is no joy in Mudville..."* Nahanni Johnston and Matthew Del Negro co-star as an unhappy young couple worn by his loss of former baseball stardom and torn by sacrifices she made for his career. As he settles into a day job working for an old high-school classmate, domestic abuse erupts. It's the bewildered husband who is the victim, enduring verbal abuse, drug-induced sexual manipulation, and beatings before he threatens to report her attacks to the authorities. Too late! *"What are you going to tell them, huh? That your little old wife beat you up?,"* she taunts, *"Big jock like you?... No, the law's on my side."* Before you can say *"three strikes and you're out!,"* she has hubby on the ropes as the mounting bloodshed escalates toward its inevitable conclusion.

I'd like to say genre expectations are turned on their head, but this is old-hat stuff. Such gender-reversal mayhem was fresh when Clint Eastwood made his directorial debut with *Play Misty for Me* back in 1971, but after the plethora of similar fare in the wake of *Fatal Attraction*'s megahit status, this became pretty tried-and-true 'fe-

---

[56] As mentioned in the introduction, a slightly revamped 'bastardized' edit of this review was published, sans payment or even a single comp copy, in *Rue Morgue* magazine (#38, March/April 2004, archived at http://www.joao-machado.com/clippings/clippings_en.htm). It was my one and only published piece in that zine, and will remain so.

male-psycho' turf in the 1990s: see *Single White Female* and recent direct-to-vid Bs like *Malicious, The Perfect Wife*, etc.

That said, this psycho-thriller is well-made and played, building a compelling cast of characters and considerable tension before settling into a genre groove familiar to most contemporary video renters and viewers. The engaging depiction of the wife's slide from disappointment to despair before homicide erupts is at its best in the first third of the film, promising a stronger drama than the dip into genre conventions delivers (including the final, EC-Comics style twist, which was taboo-busting in the 1950s but is weak tea in 2002). In many ways, the central sequence set in and around the high-school reunion is the film's key sequence, powerfully conveying the spiral of internalized emotions at work; as the scenario decisively shifts into thriller mode after the reunion, it fails to sustain the clarity and insights of this scene and all that led up to it.

Kane's direction is stronger than his script (which is, despite my criticism, deftly constructed), boasting crisp production and visual values while coaxing convincing performances throughout, particularly from the two leads. Alan Pottinger scores as the sleazy high-school-classmate-as-boss who indulges malingering animosities toward his alma mater's prize couple, savoring the cruelest twists of black humor Kane's script offers before he reaches a suitably nasty end.

[This was a disappointment for me, perhaps due to my own familiarity with the given genre. But that will be a plus, not a liability, in most retail venues hungry for solid thriller product, where the film's close-enough-for-comfort Play Misty for Me/Fatal Attraction *derivation will attract its target audience. Nothing really different*

here, but as I say, that's probably going to ultimately serve this feature well in the marketplace. Thus, a strong contender for the final selection, though I personally prefer other films in this batch.]

MOLE (2001; Scr/Dir: Richard Mauro and Anthony Savini) Fine suspense drama set beneath Manhattan, in the long-abandoned tunnels legendary for their unexplored depths and the homeless and 'creatures' purported to live there. Mauro and Savini's script plays off that reputation to slowly mount an unnerving war-of-nerves between a trio (an eager-to-advance newscaster, her cameraman, and a 'expert' on the underground acting as their guide) who brave the darkness in search of a story – the identity of a possible killer, responsible for unidentified remains found in the area.

The narrative is a familiar one – the Pre-Code horror comic *Mr. Mystery* featured a corker of a 'monsters in the subway' story back in 1953, Gary Sherman directed the gem of the form in 1972 with the UK-made *Death Line*, aka *Raw Meat*, and the filmmakers herein acknowledge (with a line of dialogue) the 1984 precursor horror flick *C.H.U.D.*[57] – but *Mole* stays true to its own path. Mauro and Savini provide solid enough scripting and helming to carry the day, and a thin premise that could have been just another *Blair Witch* wanna-be quickly establishes and maintains its own distinctive tenor and terror, thanks in part to the solid performances and clever twist in the tail. Most of all, the feature is distinguished by co-scenarist/director Anthony ("Bluebeard") Savini's photography and the decision to film in the actual NYC subterranean tunnels. One can only

---

[57] The UK feature *Creep* (2004) was another of this breed.

wonder what the filmmaking team endured to commit this to film/video... therein, no doubt, lays another tale. Recommended!

Strong packaging and word-of-mouth could make this a real sleeper on the video shelves; let's hope this comes to market soon![58]

OCEAN PARK (2001; Dir/Scr: David Warfield; 101 min.): Compelling contemporary noir travels a well worn path but works thanks to a clever, tightly-wound script, solid direction, and an excellent cast.

On-the-skids actor Wilson Enfield (Kenneth Hughes) becomes a prime suspect in a murder investigation when a down-on-her-luck aspiring actress Jolette (Alexandra Wilson) he worked with is found strangled in her apartment. When Jolette's twin sister (also played by Wilson) appears to claim the body and push for answers, Enfield's dubious involvement and attempt to play other involved parties against one another (including his Hollywood star brother-in-law, caught in rough sex play with the victim on a video Enfield has secreted away, and a cop whose unrequited affections for Jolette is more than a bit obsessive) edges him into danger. But he doesn't deviate from the task at hand, drawing himself and those in the victim's orbit into increasingly desperate extremes...

---

[58] Ironically, the two features I liked the least of those I previewed – *Parasite* and *R.I.C.C.O.* – were the first to land distribution with existing labels and make it to market. *The Young Unknowns* played in a few urban markets and was released on DVD in 2006, while *Boom, Rutland, U.S.A.*, and others were self-distributed by their respective filmmakers.

The entire film is fueled by the utter conviction of the creators and performers, with Hughes and particularly Wilson real standouts in their roles. Crisp cinematography and locations are also a plus, matching the feature's psychological and emotional labyrinth with atmospheric setpieces (including genre staples like the city morgue and an extended sequence beneath a pier as the tide rises). As usual with this genre, the ride is more engaging than the downbeat destination, but Warfield struts his stuff with style and rigorous attention to the narrative and characters above all; he is a talent to watch, as is Wilson. Recommended!

PARASITE (1997; Dir/Scr: Patrick Roddy): Well-crafted and potentially unnerving scenario succumbs to lackluster treatment in this throwback to the early-'80s direct-to-video horror mold. Writer/director Patrick Roddy clearly has talent and skill, but unlikable cast of characters and players, so-so technical credits, and sluggish pace make this a limp genre outing.

The premise – an arrogant university professor is undone by paranormal events he at first scoffs at – was initiated by the great Fritz Lieber tale *Conjure Wife* back in the 1940s (brought to the screen twice; the second adaptation – Sidney Hayers' *Burn, Witch, Burn*; original UK title: *Night of the Eagle*, 1961 – remains one of the finest genre sleepers of the 1960s). As in Lieber's tale, a male professor (microbiologist Richard Austin, played by David Gaffney) suffers the insidious supernatural influence of an elder, physically-crippled female 'witch' (here, the mesmerist Miss Vohich, played by Julia Matias); in Roddy's script, Vohich seeks not to destroy her prey, but to claim him as her mate, her malignant influence detouring into bloodshed only after he spurns her.

This overtly sexual angle might have worked, had there been any appeal whatsoever in the characters or performers. Alas, we neither like nor care about what might happen to this unpleasant cast, and the real mayhem – when it finally comes, late in the game, via razor blades and an axe – isn't energetic or malicious enough to rouse much interest. Furthermore, the sluggish pacing only emphasizes the essentially dour nature of the characters and proceedings. This is among the most morose horror films ever made, to its detriment.

Photography is merely okay and too often murky, while audio is often poor; nonetheless, Roddy does mount some compelling sequences (the harrowing title sequence; effective cross-cutting during the love-making scenes undone by visions of demon talons and literal baths in blood) that indicate he's capable of much better work, given an engaging cast and greater means.

RADIO FREE STEVE (2000; Dir/Scr: Jules Beesley; 82 min.): I'm sure this plays best with a rowdy, packed, sympathetic film festival audience who can readily embrace the conceit (that what we are watching is a 'found relic' of 1984 indy filmmaking) and calculatedly raucous, slipshod nature of this redneck Texan sf comedy. It's racked up an impressive track record on the festival circuit, but this puppy left me cold, save for a few amusing moments.

The fictional 'hook' of the film is that in 1999, international director "Lars von Biers" (nyuk nyuk nyuk) discovered and 'brought to light' a 'lost' unfinished video feature, *Radio Free Steve*, purportedly made in 1984 by Scott Glenn (playing himself with initially convincing elan). That established, the 'restored' *Radio Free Steve* unreels, tracking the exploits of its titular hero, a post-apocalypse guerrilla radio broadcaster, the *"one lone pirate"* to survive into the new Millennium. Mobile-broadcasting his brain dead screeds in a mutant-mashing van while eluding determined FCC assassin Dirk Suxx (Chris Sykes), Steve races beneath crudely-solarized Western skies while alternately idolizing and insulting his wench Sheena (Jessy Schwartz) in classic 'Texist-sexist' style. When Steve catches a glimpse of an underground TV music video broadcast, he sets off on a quest for its source, encountering mutants, 'wastelanders,' radioactive beer, and visiting a 'Hippie Farm' before he endures the climactic breakdance arena competition and poolside debauchery of L.A.

Though he's short, loud, and has brass balls, Steve Glenn isn't charismatic enough to carry the antics, despite the procession of bad haircuts he suffers. The 'von Biers' dig – reference to the Dogme 95 scene – and a *Blair Witch* parodic shot cues us to one of the many targets of writer/director Beesley's satire, but the shotgun approach soon wears thin as we realize there is no real point to the proceedings save its good-ol'-boy *"Fuck You"* attitude, which the viewer will find either hopelessly ingratiating or aggravating; for those who share the 'tude, that'll be enough to make this a winner.

In the end, *Radio Free Steve* proves ultimately less entertaining than the trashy post-apocalyptic Italian *Mad Max* ripoffs it lampoons, succumbing to numbing banter, unfunny in-jokes, and its rambling, ramshackle beer-guzzling nonsense. Since the era of Larry Buchanan, lots of Texans have made plenty of drop-dead serious impoverished exploitationers in this mold that are just as bad as *Radio Free Steve*, and inadvertently funnier. For my money, Firesign Theater's superficially similar vein of satire was denser, deeper, and far, far funnier, but all that may prove is that 'head humor' works best without a six-pack and a fifth to deaden the nerves. Nevertheless, Beesley's pic would be a steady renter for youths and the less discriminating cult crowd seeking cheap thrills, and it sure would rent in Texas; the cameo from *X-Files* 'Lone Gunman' Dean Haglund only enhances that cult status. (Sigh) – If I'd seen this when I was 21 or under, I'm sure I'd have loved it, too.

R.I.C.C.O. (2002; Dir/Scr: Shawn Woodard, Marcus Canty; 105 min.): Maladroit urban crime 'thriller' lacks thrills or drive. Static script, direction, playing, and poor technical credits (further aggravated by the shoddy quality of the EP screener) add up to tedium occasionally enlivened only by bloody onscreen gunplay.

Lawyer Wesley Wallaceson (Walter Harris) stumbles onto a 'snatch' and rescues fugitive Naomi (Sophia Taylor) from a pair of thugs who casually blast their way through various cat-and-mouse antics at the behest of the mysterious 'Ricco.' Offscreen Ricco orders kidnapping, torture, and murder with impunity, but good help is hard to find these days, and Wallaceson eventually uncovers his true identity after much folderol.

Though the effort is commendable, there really isn't anything to recommend here, not even the lurid highlights typical of the urban cops & crooks genre. The staple car chase is abbreviated to a single shot and Wallaceson's offscreen voiceover describing his escape; other escapes occur offscreen; despite talk of prostitution and the inevitable bed-down between Wallaceson and Naomi, there's no sexual antics; and so on. Not even the occasional risible lines – *"How can a panty-wearing lawyer cause me so much grief?"* or *"Get Mr. Tan on the phone... then inject him with number five"* – aren't enough to get a rise out of this crudely filmed, humdrum by-the-numbers fare.

RIFFED (2001; Dir: Lorenzo Gabriele; script by Gabriele and Francisco Lorite; 95 min.): *Dilbert* meets Walter Mitty in this okay, arch black comedy-of-manners spoofing corporate office conformity, which ultimately restyles the old Hercules hydra myth (cut off one head, and two grow) for the WTO era in which all workers are expendable.

Film opens with a lyrical 'early retirement' sequence – an unhappy employee's 200+ stories dive to the sidewalk – which opens the door for Spencer Blank (played by writer/producer Francisco Lorite) to join the work force of Global Corp. In short order, the division Spencer works with is rattled by the intrusion of a *"re-engineering facilitator"* pro named Hackman (Sean Cullin), engaged by Global to force the team into the 'productivity zone' with dubious 'team-building' exercises, unintelligible graphs, 'down-sizing' psycho babble, and enigmatic one-on-one confrontations with Spencer and his co-workers. The frustrations and fears of individuality versus the 'hive' mentality demanding by corporate environments mount to absurdist extremes, punctuated with very-human bouts of sex in the copy room, suspicions, browbeating, pecking-order dynamics, and Spencer's Walter Mitty-like fantasies of power and retribution.

The stripped-down execution (essentially the six cast members, existing in a cartoonish vacuum) intermittently works, but becomes an ultimately sterile artifice that undermines the film by its second half. The feeling that there *is* no world outside the chosen Global Corp office should work in the film's favor, but the cumulative lack of any details beyond the increasingly desperate dynamic between the principles becomes a liability rather than a strength as the events continue to move into expected narrative grooves. Similar subject matter was handled in Mike Judge's *Office Space* and Jill Sprecher's *Clockwatchers* to better effect, without plunging their respective scenarios into such a crippling, unreal 'twilight zone.'

That said, Lorenzo Gabirele's direction is assured throughout, and the ensemble cast is good, with Stanley Harrison quietly delivering the standout performance as the elder worker Sydney Martin. Kudos to Shawn Kim's cinematography and especially Thierry Malet's musical score, which is excellent.

ROPE ART (2002; Dir/Scr: Thomas Griffith; 93 min.): A fictional confrontation between moralist authorities and sexual performance artists in Dade County, Florida erupts into controversy and culminates in violence in this earnest but labored, schematic melodrama.

Jockeying for an issue to build his political campaign upon, Assistant D.A. Marty Jensen (John Dark Walters) embraces a hard-right Christian moralist agenda and prosecutes various 'sinful' establishments in his community, rousing the populace and media while alienating his lawyer wife Carrie (Micah West). Carrie's boredom with Marty and their marriage sends her into the night life, gravitating to the exotic bondage performance artist Thomas Yanari (Alan Moor), which in turn sends Marty seeking comfort with his female coworker and – disastrously – a prostitute. While Carrie and Yanari cultivate their own consensual bondage-based relations, she also takes on the civil liberties case pressed by her husband, setting the stage for the film's procedural courtroom polemic.

Writer/director Thomas Griffith wears his convictions on his sleeve throughout, mounting a provocative enough situation that is ultimately defused by its creaky narrative mechanics and straight-laced dramaturgy that becomes increasingly risible. West and Moor carry their roles fairly well, but Walters is a disaster as the weak-chinned, priggish Jensen; of the Nick Adams/David Duchovny mold, Walters humorlessly shuffles through his role without a spark of life or conviction. Technical credits are okay, but nothing exceptional visually, and the audio and editing are only passable.

The sex – never explicit, though there are stretches of nudity, elaborate bondage, and an erect penis pops up in one bondage shot – hasn't a spark of life to it, either. The arch dialogue doesn't help matters: Yanari: *"What do you think?"* Carrie: *"My brain just crashed!"* After introducing Carrie to the excitement of tame (but elaborately knotted) sadomasochistic bondage (handing her a rope and a handy photocopied instructional pamphlet!), Yanari trusses up Carrie and asks, *"How do you feel?"* Carrie replies, *"Sexy – very turned on – frightened,"* in deadpan monotone. Given a little more juice in either the erotic or satiric direction, these scenes might have worked, but fail in either the Radley Metzger or Russ Meyer camps. Once the sexual shenanigans give way completely to the clash of shaky regional obscenity laws and constitutional rights in the dry, protracted final act in the courtroom (a detour that even derailed Russ Meyer in his heyday: see, or don't see, *The Seven Minutes*), *Rope Art* looses what little steam it musters en route.

RUTLAND, U.S.A. (2002; Dir: Chad Meserve; script by Meserve and Jon Artigo; 94 min.): Pleasant autumn settings and a 'Bobcat Scout' troop earnestly applying 'last aid' to a stray corpse found in the woods (an effective rip of the infamous *National Lampoon* magazine parody) kick off this okay but overlong regional comedy feature set and shot in the real-life village of Rutland, Massachusetts.

Rutland, we're told by a cable-access news anchor woman investigating the nonsensical murder-mystery at the core of the film, *"lies at the exact center of the state."* The implication is, of course, that Rutland embodies the current state of 'normality' in dysfunctional small-town America. Here, father-and-son relations are defined by exhibitionism, *"inappropriate urination,"* sexual humiliation, and voyeurism; a barely-literate high school science teacher clumsily plots to kidnap his loveliest student for ransom; and the tabloid aspirations of the cable access news anchor are stymied by her loutish brother who 'needs' her editing equipment to play video games. Some of the comic conceits score (a domestic violence group-therapy session in which participants are instructed that in public, hands are to be slapped; in private, faces) and some broad gags and comedic characters are funny, but it's a hit-or-miss, hit-and-run affair whose leisurely pace ultimately works against it.

A synopsis of the loosely-knit, calculatedly ramshackle narrative and ensemble of quirky local performers suggests Todd Solondz territory (*Welcome to the Dollhouse, Happiness, Storytelling*), but the film is initially closer to the offbeat charms of Alfred Hitchcock's *The Trouble With Harry* (which likewise spun an oddball cast in orbit around a misplaced corpse in a pastoral New England fall setting) before its antics shift into overt silliness with its incompetent detective, kidnap-caper slapstick, and even a tights-wearing vigilante hero. This transparently good-natured absurdist affair plays its black comedy for whimsy instead of outrage, comfortable with dancing around its cavalcade of rural perversions for chuckles, but it's essentially toothless. There's no real bite or laughs, though the potential is there.

Contemporary television sitcoms habitually tread similar ground these days and the current phase of Hollywood scatological all-star comedies revel in grosser excesses, robbing *Rutland, U.S.A.* of any distinction as either a comedy or a feature. That said, the filmmakers show obvious skill, talent, and the promise for better work in the future, and their accompanying trailer and demo reel demonstrates considerable experience. *Rutland, U.S.A.* is a well-crafted regional effort that would benefit from a brisker pace and tighter comedic timing, a slight confection that is likable but hardly memorable as either a comedy or an indy.

[Note: Please do *watch the trailer reel, which is enclosed with the feature. After the teaser and trailer for* Rutland, USA, *there's an enchanting stop-motion animated short entitled* Rex & Red *that I recommend viewing. Check it out!]*

SHOOTING BLANKS (2002; Dir/Scr: Davor Dirlic; 75 min.): Revisionist film noir has been fashionable among indies since *Blue Velvet* and *Blood Simple* revamped the genre for the 1980s and *Pulp Fiction* kicked it into overdrive for the 1990s. From Australia comes the deadpan tale of geeky wannabe filmmaker Max Perich (Wayne Hope) who, after losing his job at the local grocery for tending to fruitless 'pitch' lunches instead of work, accidentally rear-ends a parked car. Out struts wannabe-actress Roma Calamari (Tess Masters), whom Max seizes on as the key to launching his planned serial killer feature. It's bad enough that Max's roommate punk brother (and punk girlfriend) drag him into their petty robberies, and that he stumbles into a marshland execution that seems to have been lifted from his script, but red-headed femme fatale Roma soon derails Max into a dead-end tour of Melbourne's urban underbelly punctuated with extortion, sex, violence, and murder.

Writer-director Davor Dirlic's parody-noir brings its potboiler narrative to a proper head of steam with arch dialogue, caricaturish performances, and pop flair, favoring bright primary colors in its cinematography (by Simeon Bryan) and production design (by Christiane Hanesch). In the first few minutes, Max's bright yellow vehicle crunches Roma's sky-blue crate, establishing the film's 'live-action cartoon' palette, spiced throughout with *giallo* flourishes. There are plenty of nods to its chosen genre (including an *Eraserhead* poster prominent on Max's kitchen wall to acknowledge Dirlic's debt to David Lynch), but *Shooting Blanks* manages to establish and maintain its own footing en route.

It's lovely to look at and clicks along at a brisk pace, boasting a few funny twists in the final bloody act, though the deliberately flat characterizations (as stylized and two-dimensional as the film's 'look') take a toll. Some viewers will find Max an insufferable dweeb, the rest of the cast utterly unsympathetic, and the film aptly titled; he is, they are, and it is – which is, of course, much of the joke. If you're along for the ride, *Shooting Blanks* is an engaging curio. As a rental item, it could do very well if properly packaged and promoted with a self-deprecating panache reflective of the film itself.

THE YOUNG UNKNOWNS (2000; Scr/Dir: Catherine Jelski; 87 min.): Underrated actor Devon Gummersall (from TV's *My So-Called Life*, and most recently on video in *Earth vs. The Spider*) anchors this feature, starring as Charlie Foxx, an aspiring actor whose life in the gutters of L.A.'s fringe subculture is sliding ever so steadily town the toilet. Adrift in a haze of drugs and drink, his addictive misbehavior has finally done in his relationship with his girlfriend Paloma (Arly Jover), who works (as a production coordinator) in the industry Charlie so aches to be a part of.

Though the events are, ultimately, catastrophic, this is essentially a character-driven tone poem, sustaining a saturated atmosphere of gloomy despair most similar films flinch from, or shatter with melodramatic overstatement. Adapting her debut feature from a play (*"Magic Afternoon"* by Wolfgang Bauer), writer and director Catherine Jelski fleshes out the almost anecdotal situation into a surprisingly resonant snapshot of twenty-somethings' life on the edge of affluence. Cut off from his parents (his father consumed with career in faraway London, his mother retreating into alcoholism and despair in faraway Vermont) and maxed-out on his credit cards, Charlie's narcissism, casual misogyny (which rudely asserts itself whenever he is in the presence of his white wannabe-'gangsta' friend Joe, convincingly played by Eion Bailey), and increasing disregard for anyone or thing outside of himself slithers into increasingly callous and self-destructive behavior after he receives grave news about his mother. The swaggering facade erodes, Paloma finally makes her departure, and there is nothing left to avert the downward spiral of events.

Gabor Szitanyi's cinematography and editing are bright and resonant, Hypnogaja's musical score is ideal, and the top-drawer cast of young pseudo-unknowns are perfectly attuned to the reality of Jelski's script and direction. Leslie Bibb is particularly affecting as the unfortunate Lassandra, whose transformation from a sassy, picture-perfect model to a broken, terrified waif caught in the uncaring orbit of Charlie and Joe's vacuum proves the most heartbreaking character arc of all. Recommended.

[This will be a tough rental in some markets; though similar to Hurlyburly, Bully *and others, the lack of star power may not balance out the decidedly downbeat nature of the film. That said, this is a very strong independent, assured and measured, and will benefit if appropriately packaged and promoted to its target audience.]*[59]

---

[59] This review – and at least one other from this section, perhaps *Mole* – were published in Steven Puchalski's excellent zine *Shock Cinema*. At the time of this writing, my file copies of *Shock Cinema* are out of reach; rest assured, I will cover this in an upcoming volume of *Gooseflesh*, and include all specs (issue and page numbers, etc.) in that volume. See http://www.shockcinemamagazine.com/backissues.html

VMag Extras:

The Score Score[60]

If space permitted, I'd rhapsodize over film composers Nino Rota, John Barry, Goblin, Carter Burwell, Michael Nyman, Howard Shore, Danny Elfman and others. Precious few of the current breed, however, measure up to the standards established by the five listed alphabetically here:

1. Angelo Badalamenti: His earliest scores were credited to 'Andy Badale' (*Gordon's War*, 1973; *Law and Disorder*, 1974). Blossoming during his collaborations with director David Lynch, Badalamenti's *Blue Velvet* (1986; score on CD, Varese Sarabande #VCD47277)[61] was evocative but fairly conventional, hardly preparing audiences for the intoxicating ranges of *Twin Peaks* (1990; Warner #9 26316-2) and its feature companion *Twin Peaks: Fire Walk With Me* (1992; Warner #9 45019-2). Spillover collaborations between Badalamenti and Lynch include two Julee Cruise albums (*Floating*

---

[60] This was originally published as my part of *"Top 5 Musicals, Musicians and Soundtrack Composers"* in *VMag* #2, the *'Music'* issue, December 1997, pp. 17-18; the other entries accompanying my lists were *"5 Musicals Which G. Michael Dobbs Enjoys"* and *"Bill and Dana: ..You Know They've Gotta Helluva Band."* Note this issue of *VMag* also featured my article *"Oh Captain, My Captain: An Ode to Captain Beefheart, Daddy of Diddy Wah Dada,"* pp. 10-11.

[61] Note, please, all the CD and vinyl information in this article is over a decade old, and hence out of date; online searches for more current availability and pressings are essential.

Into the Night and *The Voice of Love*), one very bizarre performance piece, *Industrial Symphony No. 1: The Dreams of the Broken Hearted* (1990; on Warner Home Video #38179-3), and the recent *Lost Highway* (1997; my least favorite). The eclectic composer has also scored other visionary features (*The City of Lost Children/La Cité des Enfants Perdus*, 1995, etc.) and recently collaborated with Tim Booth on *Booth and the Bad Angel* (Mercury #314526 852-2), all highly recommended.

2. Elmer Bernstein: Not to be confused with master conductor Leonard (who also composed scores, including *On the Waterfront* and *West Side Story*), at his best Elmer Bernstein is the Aaron Copeland of cinema. His inventive early film scores included (no shit) *Robot Monster* and *Cat Women of the Moon* (both 1953). His most renowned work includes the archetypal scores for *The Magnificent Seven* (1960; revamped to become the signature for Marlboro cigarette TV ads), *The Great Escape* (1963), on through to *Age of Innocence* (1993) and more. To my mind, his finest score was *To Kill a Mockingbird* (1962). This rich and profoundly moving slice of Americana was recently rerecorded by the maestro himself, complete with cues that didn't make the final cut of the film (Varese Sarabande #VSD-5754). [62]

3. Bernard Herrmann: Perhaps the most shamelessly imitated of all film composers, Herrmann matched the bravado, bravery and vision of directors like Orson Welles and Alfred Hitchcock beat for beat, stroke for stroke, consistently forging a profound wedding of ci-

---

[62] Note that Bernstein passed away on August 18, 2004, with over 240 movie scores to his credit.

nema and music. Herrmann also lent his considerable talents to many 'lesser' but no less exciting productions, from the original *Cape Fear* (1962) and Ray Harryhausen's finest fantasy films to TV series like *The Twilight Zone* (1959-63). A new generation of directors kept him busy until his death, yielding the brooding scores for Martin Scorsese's *Taxi Driver* (1976), Brian DePalma's *Sisters* (1973) and *Obsession* (1976), and more. *Any* Herrmann score is well worth owning and hearing time and time again, but be sure to get your hands on the originals and/or Herrmann's own recordings. Don't miss the primary Hitchcock trilogy: *Vertigo* (1958; recently remastered on Varese Sarabande #VSD-5759), *North by Northwest* (1959; Turner/Rhino #R272101), and *Psycho* (1960; the Herrmann-conducted original score is only on vinyl, though a new Varese Sarabande CD features a newly-restored version conducted by Joel McNeely). Also worth tracking down is the excellent biography, *A Heart at Fire's Center: The Life and Music of Bernard Herrmann* by Steven C. Smith (1991, University of California Press).

4. Krzysztof (Christopher) Komeda: Jazz musician Komeda made his mark internationally scoring fellow Pole Roman Polanski's short films and key 1960s features (except *Repulsion*, 1965), breaking into mainstream American theaters with his exquisite, haunting score for *Rosemary's Baby* (1968). Sadly, Komeda died from complications following an untreated head injury in 1968, and his work has yet to be rediscovered. Precious little of it is available on vinyl or CD (I'm told there are jazz recordings available from Poland), though recently remastered video and laserdisc releases of Polanski's early masterpieces may pique your interest.

Komeda's playful, evocative and ominous choral arrangements for *The Fearless Vampire Killers* (1967, MGM/UA) is particularly recommended.

5. Ennio Morricone: Arguably the most inventive and prolific[63] of all contemporary film composers, Morricone's vast body of work is readily available. Be selective, avoid the pop reorchestrations by lesser composers/conductors; original recordings only, please. His ground-breaking compositions for Sergio Leone's classic films are required listening: *A Fistful of Dollars* (*Per un Pugno di Dollari*, 1964), *For a Few Dollars More* (*Per Qualche Dollaro in Più*, 1965; both on *Ennio Morricone: The Legendary Italian Westerns*, BMG/RCA #9974-2-R), *The Good, The Bad and the Ugly* (*Il Buono, Il Brutto, Il Cattivo*, 1966; Capital #48408), *Once Upon a Time in the West* (*C'era una Volti il West*, 1968; the finest of all: BMG/RCA #4736-2-R), *Duck, You Sucker* (aka *A Fistful of Dynamite; Giù la Testa*, 1971; complete on *An Ennio Morricone Western Quintet*, DRG #32907), and *Once Upon a Time in America* (1984; Mercury #822 334-2). My favorite contemporary Morricone scores, *Rampage* (1988) and *Casualties of War* (1989), are on vinyl but not yet, to my knowledge, on CD. Morricone's personal favorite of his recent scores, *The Mission* (1986, Virgin #V2-86001), is also recommended.

My favorite contemporary scores on CD? It's quite a fruit cocktail. Aside from those listed above, they are, listed alphabetically by title:

---

[63] As of this book's publication, Morricone has scored almost 500 films, and is still very active as a composer.

1. *Akira* (1988; score released 1990; JVC #JMI-1001) A fantastic, one-of-a-kind score. Geinoh Yamashirogumi's irresistible score for Katsuhiro Otomo's seminal science-fiction anime masterpiece literally opens like a nuclear blast, subsequently building upon choral and percussion arrangements quite alien to western ears.

2. *Blade Runner* (1982; 1994, Atlantic #82623-2) Vangelis' now-classic science-fiction noir composition has *finally* been rescued from oblivion, resurrected by the composer and interwoven with memorable (though somewhat intrusive) dialogue clips from the film. Avoid the earlier recording (still on CD) at all costs – the authorized Atlantic CD listed here is the one to get.

3. *Cal* (1984; *Music by Mark Knopfler from the film Cal*, Mercury #822 769-2) Along with Danny Elfman (of Oingo Boingo: see below) and Steward Copeland (formerly of The Police), Dire Straits veteran Knopfler is one of the few pop composers to bring a distinctive and appropriate talent to contemporary cinema. Knopfler's done some great scores (*Local Hero,* 1983, *The Princess Bride,* 1987, etc.), and there's a fine collection of his work available on CD (*Screenplaying,* Warner #9 45457-2), but his spare, heartfelt score for Cal remains his finest.

4. *Cannibal Holocaust* (1980; 1995, Lucertola Media #LMCD 003, limited edition 1000 copies) No, this is not a joke! This is one of the most beautiful film scores ever composed, alternating between lush romanticism and a raw-nerved threnody. Riz Ortolani scored the notorious documentary *Mondo Cane* (1962), complimenting some of the most odious images of '60s cinema with *"More"* (which won the Grammy Award and an Academy Award nomination for "Best Song" of 1962). He worked the same perverse magic for Cannibal Holocaust, one of the most reprehensibly explicit of all modern horror films. Ortolani also scored *The Yellow Rolls Royce* (1964) and *Brother Sun, Sister Moon* (*Fratello Sole, Sorella Luna*, 1972), among over 200 others, but this is his best.

5. *Forbidden Zone* (1980; 1990, Varese Sarabande #VSD-5268) I love all of Danny Elfman's soundtracks, but Elfman and the Mystic Knights of the Oingo Boingo's debut score for brother Richard Elfman's Fleischer Brothers-cartoon-on-acid midnight movie is a giddy delight. Elfman speed-blenders Cab Calloway, Miguelito Valdez, the Kipper Kids and Herve Villechaize (!) into a cool whip confection for the ears. *"Oi, vey, the Yiddishe Charleston!"*

Video Virgin Pix:
Top Ten Turn-Ons (and Turn-Offs)[64]

What turns you on? What turns you off? And can you rent it, tonight, at your local video store? Jeez, how should we know? But we sure know what we *like and*

---

[64] Originally published in *VMag* #4, the *'Over-Sexed Valentine's Day Special,'* February 1998, pp. 21-25; the issue also featured my daughter Maia's first published short story, *"A Plastic Kind of Day"* (pg. 8). Given *Blur*'s format, I have added the respective film release years for this article reprint, though I only listed that information with the respective 'top ten' items in the original version.

don't like, and here's our current list of video sex dos and don'ts...

Sex is such a subjective thing – in fact, it's probably the most subjective thing in the world. It's tough recommending 'turn-on' titles, because it's different for everybody, really. Mind you, sex isn't necessarily something involving romance, or even romantic. That *can* get in the way for some folks, you see.

Even between friends, lovers, partners, or long-married couples, it's damn near impossible to agree on one movie that was a total turn-on for both consenting adults, much less compile a top-ten list. Depending on age, attitudes and sexual orientation, we'd all compile lists that are light years apart.

And that, you see, is where the fun begins.

For openers, let's forget about *Boogie Nights* (1997) and *Deep Throat* (1972) and *Oriental Anal Whores IV* (1997), just for a moment. For the purposes of the next couple of paragraphs, let's just narrow the field to one middle-class, middle-age hetero couple who rents at Blockbuster, shall we? Okay.

For instance, she gets wet watching Susan Sarandon getting her toenails polished by Kevin Costner in *Bull Durham* (1988; the only baseball movie she'll watch, and now you know why). He could care less. Give him Kathleen Turner having her way with stupid lawyer William Hurt in *Body Heat* (1981), though, and he's raring to go. He wants to hit the pause button and climb in the sack immediately after Sharon Stone crosses her legs during the interrogation scene in *Basic Instinct* (1992); she could care less about that flash of pink, give her Brad Pitt showing Geena Davis how it's done in *Thelma*

& Louise (1991) – forget the pause button, let's rewind and watch it two more times. While she's turned on by Harvey Keitel's finger probing the hole in Holly Hunter's stocking in *The Piano* (1993), even the thought of Keitel naked turns him off – hey, can't we watch Michael Douglas and Glenn Close going at it in the kitchen in *Fatal Attraction* (1987) instead?

She swoons at *Dirty Dancing* (1987), he craves the softcore Euro-Oriental couplings of *The Lover* (*L'Amant*, 1992). She's eyeing the Daniel Day Lewis section; he's fondling the women's prison movies. He's walking to the check-out counter with *Nine ½ Weeks* (1986), she's already rented *An Officer and a Gentleman* (1982) – for the umpteenth time.

You get the idea.

If our imaginary couple gets *really* adventurous and decides to rent something they've never heard of from that alternative video store in town, they're torn between checking out the explicit sexual obsession on view in Nagisa Oshima's *In the Realm of the Senses* (*Ai No Corrida*, 1976) or the amorous snails getting slippery in *Microcosmos* (1996). It's a bit like ordering from a foreign restaurant menu – I mean, what if they accidentally chose something as indigestible as Pier Paolo Pasolini's *Salo* (*Salò o le 120 Giornate di Sodoma*, 1975)? Whoa – *that* would sure put a crimp in the evening. Why not just relax to *Pretty Woman* (1990), or watch Tom Cruise and Rebecca De Mornay steaming up the train in *Risky Business* (1983)? Hey, that's something they can usually both agree on.

You, *VMag* reader, should be more adventurous than that. Half of the fun is finding a turn-on-or-off in a film you've never heard of before. There's numerous celebrity surprises: *Out of the World*'s Maureen Flannigan going down on *Party of Five*'s Scott Wolf aroused by their escalating crime spree in *Teenage Bonnie and Klepto Clyde* (1993); Leonardo DiCaprio sodomizing David Thewlis in *Total Eclipse* (1995). There's no end to what you can find, if you really start digging.

For what it's worth, this is my list, but I'm always eager to check out some new titles. I'd love to read top-ten turn-on and turn-off lists for gay and/or lesbian couples, but I couldn't write one, middle-aged hetero father of two that I am (there, now you know my orientation, if it isn't self-evident from my selections). Having occasionally sampled the plentiful 1990s crop of direct-to-video XXX porn, I can't say I've ever seen a single title I'd recommend from the adult room. Besides, if you frequent the video store adult room, you don't need my help indulging your particular (or peculiar) turn-ons and turn-offs. Chances are the ludicrous titles I crack up over or the box art that has me flinching has you digging in your pocket for a quick rental.[65]

The turn-offs are equally subjective. Necrophiles might love *Nekromantik*, coprophiliacs revel in select passages (no pun intended) of *The Cook, The Thief, His Wife and Her Lover* (1989) or *Salo*, but I'm fairly confident most readers will agree with the turn-offs I've arrived at. Truth to tell, the John Bobbitt video[66] should

---

[65] I was in fact manager of the adult video room at First Run Video during this period, and remained the adult video room buyer well into 2003. We had the best classic XXX section in New England. Though I barely remember most of the tsunami of adult videos I dealt with weekly, I do recall the most insane titles – prominent among those *Stop! My Ass is On Fire!*

[66] At the time this article was published, this reference needed no explanation. On the night of June 23, 1993, in Manassas, Virginia, John Wayne Bobbitt reportedly raped his wife after

have made the 'turn off' list, and bigtime. *Brrrr.* God, that was almost as bad as watching the hideous albino 'cowman' freak in the Frankenstein's monster mask get a handjob from Sylvia Miles in Tobe Hooper's *The Funhouse* (1981), or that damned blood-drinking penis pop out of the vagina-like orifice that grew in Marilyn Chambers' armpit in David Cronenberg's *Rabid* (1977). Really, it was almost that bad.

But I digress.

Paul Verhoeven's *Showgirls* (1995) should have been on the list, too, if only for the really scary lipstick (and lip liner!) Elizabeth Berkeley and Gina Gershon wore, but it loses so much on video. When those lips were forty feet across, they were truly monstrous. Ang Lee's *The Ice Storm* (1997) will make the list once it's on video for Christine Ricci's inspired foreplay while wearing a full over-the-head rubber Richard Nixon mask. No wonder poor l'il Elisha Wood is such a space case in the movie.

But first, here's the good stuff, listed chronologically.

---

arriving home intoxicating from a wild night out; abused wife Lorena Leonor Bobbitt waited until he was asleep, and using a kitchen knife proceded to sever his penis and throw it into a field. Bobbitt's penis was reattached after nine-and-a-half hours of surgery; Lorena was arrested and found not guilty after a very public trial, and they divorced in 1995. John Bobbitt starred in two XXX adult videos, *John Wayne Bobbitt: Uncut* (1994) and *Frankenpenis* (1996). For more info, see http://en.wikipedia.org/wiki/Lorena_Bobbitt

Turn-Ons:

1. Maybe it doesn't belong on this list (it doesn't arouse me in the least), but ***Buried Treasure*** (1924?) rates as the funniest sex cartoon ever made. Most Americans think Ralph Bakshi's *Fritz the Cat* (1971) was the first 'X-rated' cartoon, but *Buried Treasure* holds the lead, chronicling the misadventures of Ever-Ready Hardon, an overendowed erect little man in search of something – *anything!* – to penetrate. Reportedly completed off-hours by animators from then-major competing studios, this energetic curio brought the playful bawdiness of the notorious 'Tijuana Bibles' to cartoon life. I first saw it in Alex de Renzy's porn anthology *A History of the Blue Movie* (1970), but it's on video as part of *The Best of the New York Erotic Film Festival* (1973) and on *Sextoons: An Erotic Animation Festival* (along with fifteen other porn-toons).

2. Maureen O'Sullivan's nude swim with Johnny Weismuller in ***Tarzan and His Mate*** (1933) is still a ravishing, breathtaking sequence, a jewel sparkling amid one of the greatest adventure movies ever made. Hollywood's early sound era classics often titillated with sexual delights and innuendos, until the censors at the Breen Office and the Catholic Legion of Decency seized control in 1934. The jungle motif wasn't just Tarzan's turf: consider Marlene Dietrich wriggling out of a gorilla costume to the beat of *"Hot Voodoo"* in *Blond Venus* (1932), or Kong peeling the clothes off Fay Wray (and smelling his fingers!) minutes before Fay fleetingly bared a breast plunging off a cliff in the one and only true *King Kong* (1933). *Tarzan and His Mate* tops them all for it casual, naturalistic sensuality.

3. Russ Meyer was one of the pioneers of the American adult film industry, and ***Lorna*** (1964) remains one of his best, busting with Erskine Caldwell-style rustic, redneck passions expressed with heady abandon. Lorna Maitland is the bored backwoods wife starved for the sex her dim hunk of a hubby can't provide. All hell breaks loose when she finds what she's looking for from an escaped convict. From the first shot of a raving preacher predicting doom, Meyer's razored camerawork and editing match Lorna's perculating drive, paving the way for his later masterpieces. *Lorna* was the first sex film I ever saw, evoking an era of magazines fathers kept hidden in dresser drawers and grimy stripper calenders in the back rooms of local gas stations, so don't trust my critical judgment – see it for yourself. I still think it holds up, so to speak.

4. Russy Meyer's ***Vixen*** (1968) would make this list simply for Erica Gavin's unforgettable fireside dance with a freshly-caught trout. Gavin galvanizes the screen throughout this brisk, bawdy sex film classic, turning a fishing expedition in the wilderness of Northern Canada into a fast and furious libido lifter. My other Meyer favorites remain *Faster Pussycat, Kill, Kill!* (1966) and *Beyond the Valley of the Dolls* (1970), though not for any 'turn on' factor – they're just two of the greatest films made in the 1960s!

5. In stark contrast to Meyer's buxom entertainments, Ken Russell's lavish adaptation of D.H. Lawrence's ***Women in Love*** (1969) was the first truly adult film about sex (and, as the title promised, love) I'd ever seen, and one of the few films I've returned to year after year

ever since. Feeling trapped in their British home village, sisters Gudrun (Glenda Jackson) and Ursula (Jennie Linden) seek romance in an era of shifting values. They reject the previous generation's repressions but are unsure of their footing as they struggle with (and against) the growing bonds with their respective lovers, brooding family-bound Gerard (Oliver Reed) and eloquent individualist Rupert (Alan Bates). There is as much talk about love as there is lovemaking, all rendered with an engaging heat and immediacy, rich with life. Russell's later ***Crimes of Passion*** (1984; unrated version only, please) is also recommended, sparked by a decidedly nastier (and funnier) 1980s deviant twist on the sexual battlegrounds between men and women. Russell returned to D.H. Lawrence source material for *The Rainbow* (1989), but it doesn't hold a candle to *Women in Love*.

6. For my money, director Nicolas Roeg has explored human sexuality with more visionary candor, honesty and clarity than any other filmmaker working in the English language. In Roeg's films, sex is (as it is in life) a primal facet of his characters' lives, and their expression, exploration and/or repression of their sexuality is central to their stories; sex (or its denial) has weight, meaning, and genuine consequences. The gender-bending bisexual romps in ***Performance*** (1970, co-directed with Donald Cammell) were intoxicating, setting the stage for Roeg's subsequent solo works. The haunting, mysterious ***Walkabout*** (1971) tells the tale of a teenage girl (Jenny Agutter) and her young brother (Roeg's son Luc Roeg, credited as 'Lucien John') saved from abandonment in the Australian Outback by a teenager aborigine (David Gulpilil) who is unable to communicate or consummate his attraction to this strange

white girl. Far more explicit was the coupling of Donald Sutherland and Julie Christie in the ultimately terrifying ***Don't Look Now*** (1973), a passionate lovemaking scene that was the heart of the film. Almost as explicit were the sex scenes between Rip Torn and his female students (one of whom playfully talks into his penis as if it were a microphone), Candy Clark and sexually-incompatible extraterrestrial David Bowie in ***The Man Who Fell to Earth*** (1976), spiced with Bowie's aching memories of truly liquid sex with his extraterrestrial wife. More earthbound – and graphic – were Theresa Russell's and Art Garfunkle's sexual encounters in ***Bad Timing: A Sensual Obsession*** (1979), Roeg's most rigorous and disturbing exploration of sexual relations gone wrong; and Theresa Russell and Rutger Hauer's sexual voodoo in ***Eureka*** (1982). *Bad Timing* wasn't Roeg's only deliberate bummer: witness (if you dare) the relentless stripping away of male sexual fantasies central to *Castaway* (1986), or the Senator's (Tony Curtis as Senator Joe McCarthy) grotty gropings with a hooker in *Insignificance* (1985), both of which belong on the 'turn offs' list below. Though all of Roeg's films are worth a look, his only recent feature I can heartily recommend in this context is ***Full Body Message*** (1996).

7. When hardcore features began to hit mainstream cinemas in the early 1970s, there was a deluge of explicit fare that has since failed to stand the test of time. Of all the groundbreakers, only ***The Devil in Miss Jones*** (1972) makes the cut. The framing story is an absolute downer, from the suicide that sets up the premise (lonely, barren woman played by Georgina Spelvin samples all the sexual experiences she denied herself during her lifetime) to the concluding *No Exit* damnation, but

there's no denying the lasting power of the vivid sex that spill off the screen for the rest of its running time.

8. Paul Verhoeven's American features have been characterized by his energetic embrace of graphic sex (*Basic Instinct, Showgirls*) and violence (*RoboCop*, 1987, *Starship Troopers*, 1997), but something has been lost in the bombast. Verhoeven's earlier Dutch features are remarkably mature works, rich with eroticism. ***Turkish Delight*** (***Turks Fruit***, 1973) remains one of the most frank and vivid portraits of young love, lust, and loss ever filmed. Rutger Hauer's charismatic star turn with on-screen partner Monique van de Ven is still electric, from their early celebratory amorous encounters to the despairing final act, as van de Ven withers and Hauer tries to aggressively take what no longer exists. Also see *Keetje Tippel* (1975), *Spetters* (1980) and *De Vierde Man/The Fourth Man* (1983) for more alluring Verhoeven delights.

9. After building his reputation with a series of elegantly conceived and beautifully produced adult features (*Carmen, Baby*, 1967, *Therese and Isabelle*, 1968, *Camille 2000*, 1969, *The Lickerish Quartet*, 1970, etc.), Radley Metzger reluctantly mounted his own hardcore productions to compete with blockbusters like *Deep Throat* and *Behind the Green Door* (1972). Working under the nom de plume 'Henry Paris,' Metzger abandoned the allegorical pretensions of his softcore films, bringing an unprecedented polish and wit to his explicit but lavishly designed, performed and photographed features. Best of all, Metzger clearly liked his characters, and wanted the audience to enjoy their pleasures, lending the hardcore sex scenes a genuine warmth despite their commercial

gloss (which is far more than can be said for 99% of the sex films on video today, which reduce all participants to the level of sweaty meat). ***The Opening of Misty Beethoven*** (1976) and ***Barbara Broadcast*** (1977) were arguably the best of the stylish lot, and they're still bracing sexual entertainments, all the more refreshing for their upscale humor and playful heat. The earlier 'Henry Paris' films were *The Private Afternoons of Pamela Mann* (1974) and *Naked Came the Stranger* (1975), and they're delicious, too.

10. Look, I really don't enjoy 'erotic thrillers,' in which a cast of cosmetically attractive but unlikeable characters go through the softcore sex moves only to completely fuck each other over in the end. It's the current distillation of film noir and the Italian *gialli*, and I find even the least of those genres more rewarding. Kathleen Turner's turn in *Body Heat* (1981) still sizzles, and John Dahl's trilogy of *Kill Me Again* (1989), *Red Rock West* (1992) and *The Last Seduction* (1994) rate high. There have been a few gems, but the most fun turn-on I've come across in this vein was Linda Fiorentino's seduction of straight-laced businessman C. Thomas Howell in a cable film you've never heard of, ***Acting on Impulse*** (1993, aka *Eyes of a Stranger*). Despite the requisite twists and turns, the sting in the tail of this erotic thriller doesn't poison the pleasures of its sex. Fiorentino's absolute control of the situation never wavers, from her feline rubbing up against puppydog Howell to the ferocity with which she tears open a prophylactic package with her teeth, prepping for center stage in Dahl's venomous *The Last Seduction*. *Seduction* is by far the better movie (and hence also recommended), but my affection for the underdog *Acting on Impulse* is undimmed.

Turn-Offs (listed alphabetically):

1. Harvey Keitel was the 1990s Jekyll & Hyde when the sensitive New Zealander who stole Holly Hunter's heart in *The Piano* (1993) gave way to the urban monster on the 'right' side of the law in Abel Ferrera's masterpiece ***Bad Lieutenant*** (1992). There's no shaking Keitel's harrowing portrait of a character struggling to keep his equilibrium while wallowing in a cesspool of police corruption, gambling, hedonism, despair and drug and sex abuse until the rape of a nun inadvertently leads him towards unexpected personal redemption. Before that perverse turn of the worm, Keitel's descent perhaps reached its nadir as he pulled over a pair of teenage girls on a vague traffic violation, letting them go only after they indulge a debasing masturbatory interlude. Ferrera and Keitel never flinch, rubbing the audience's collective noses in their (our) own voyeuristic Hyde impulses.

2. The mad doctor/dentist having his way with a female victim in ***Bloodsucking Freaks*** (1978) was the sickening centerpiece of what remains, without a doubt, the most vile, hateful misogynist film ever made. This was originally released as *The Incredible Torture Show*, which pretty much sums it up. I couldn't wash off its taint for days, and still regret seeing it. I'd say more, but I don't want to attract any further undue attention to this offal. I've already said too much. Look, I'm sorry I brought it to your attention at all. The fact that I hate it so will undoubtably provoke *one* of you to go rent the damed thing. Listen, *don't*. You *don't* need to see it. Trust me on this one. Avoid it at all costs. Really. This one's toxic.

3. Unless you're a Corey fan, Corey Feldman having onscreen sex in *Blown Away* (1992) was a stomach-turner, too. No, this *isn't* the terrorist movie with Jeff Bridges and Tommy Lee Jones (that was released in 1994) – this ersatz erotic thriller primer wed *Teen Beat* with *Basic Instinct*, starring the two Coreys, Haim and Feldman, graphically coming (of age) with *Baywatch*'s Nicole Eggert as the scheming object of their obsessions. Haim's an obnoxious brat, but he wasn't physically repugnant (this was the cusp of his 'handsome' star phase), so it's conceivable somebody somewhere might enjoy his softcore (but frequent) couplings with attractive young Eggert (in unrated and R-rated versions, thank you). However, *no* one (save his consenting real-life partners) should ever have to suffer the jarring spectacle of the toad-like Feldman banging her. It's the first and only erotic thriller climax that actually appalled me, but for all the wrong reasons. Who was the target audience for this? Underage 'Coreys' fans? Why, oh *why* did I watch it? Will I ever get it up again?

4. *Café Flesh* (1982) remains the anti-porn cult XXX movie of all time, set in a post-Apocalyptic future in which survivors are either sex-positive (they can still have sex) or sex-negative (they can't; in fact, the mere touch of another person makes them retch). Unfortunately, 99% of the population are negative, and they habituate cabaret Café Flesh, where the sexually active 1% perform onstage for the negatives and their – uh, non-pleasure. Stylish, explicit, mechanical, and thouroughly depressing, with a nagging, insulting emcee and frequent close-ups of the leering voyeur negatives, just to remind

you what the filmmakers think of you while you're watching this.

5. Bob Guccione pumped millions into making *Caligula* (1980) the porn movie of all time, and what a bloated, hideous, grand, gory, lunatic entertainment it was and is, too. Among the stellar names attached to this obscene epic were Gore Vidal, Peter O'Toole (as the screen's most syphilitic Ceasar), Sir John Gielgud (who at least had the wisdom to choose a character who kills himself in the first reel), a very young Helen Mirren and, in the most curious apex of his 1970s career arc, Malcolm McDowell. Genuine Roman delirium, part Cecil B. De-Mille Biblical scandal, part *Fellini Satyricon*, and all exploitation. There's abundant explicit onscreen sex, but its impossible to enjoy it as such amid the sordid welter of cruelty, gore, rape, incest, and inadvertent hilarity. In a moment worthy of the Marx Brothers, young Caligula orders his current sexual partner, his horse, be taken *"to the stables – I'm exhausted!"* (!!!) I love every heartless minute of it. See the X-rated version only, of course, and beware the endless procession of unrelated Caligula spin-off titles. Guccione, thank God, never made another feature.

6. It's hard to cite just one atrocity that stands out in the justifiably notorious *Ilsa* series canon, but the literally explosive climax of *Ilsa, Harem Keeper of the Oil Sheiks* (1976) was pretty high concept. The first of the series, *Ilsa, She-Wolf of the SS* (1974), opened with an unsatisfied Ilsa (Dyanne Thorne, purring with evil) castrating a male prisoner who failed to sexually satiate her, immediately placing all the exploitation cards on the table. The first sequel, *Harem Keeper of the Oil Sheiks*,

takes the cake in the turn-off department, though, with the exploding contraceptive diaphragm (!) inserted into one of the titular harem girls to dispose of the titular sheik (reportedly played, by the way, by none other than the late Spaulding Gray). The entire mid-1970s Nazi-porn epidemic (most of them made in Italy) was reprehensible, but *Ilsa* still stands tall amid the refuse.

7. American cinema is brimming with horrific rape sequences, but the almost interminable rape in ***I Spit on Your Grave*** (1977) remains the most horrific of all. Worse yet, just when you (and its victim) think it's finally over, it begins again. This film earned scathing critical scorn from none other than Siskel and Ebert, which (as it always does) scored this impoverished quickie instant notoriety. It's a primal revenge tale – a woman (Camille Keaton) seeking solitude in the countryside survives a multiple rape, eventually stalking and murdering her violators – realized with stark low-budget *cinéma vérité* immediacy. Stripped of the professional gloss Hollywood ladels over similar rape/revenge fantasies (e.g., *Lipstick, Sudden Impact*, etc.), sans even a musical score, this maladroit potboiler is humorless, grim, and devastating, and may be the most searing depiction of rape ever committed to film.[67] It was shot in Connecticut and originally released as *Day of the Woman*.

8. It's a good thing the Oklahoma City prudes who busted *The Tin Drum* (*Die Blechtrommel*, 1979) never heard of ***Leolo*** (1993). This little gem is as engaging as *The Tin Drum*, and hits even closer to home with its por-

---

[67] This is no longer true: see Gaspar Noé's *Irréversible* (2002), but be careful when you do.

trait of a boy's confused sexual explorations as he struggles to keep his sanity amid his completely insane family. Little Leolo takes a break from his compulsive writing (which provides the core and frame for the film) to spy on the lovely girl next door, who bathes and tends Leolo's lecherous grandfather. Aroused and confused, Leolo finds the fresh liver in mother's fridge an ideal masturbation aid – and doesn't say a word when mom cooks it up afterward and serves it to the family. You know, I never ate liver anyway.

9. Money for sex isn't a pretty picture, and the documentary *Mustang: House of Pleasure* (1977) deromanticized prostitution once and for all. There's no explicit sex footage here, nothing sensationalistic or scatological, just a straightforward portrait of life and labor at the Mustang, Nevada's *"biggest and best legal brothel."* Filmmaker Robert Guralnick introduces us to the owner Joe, the girls, and the johns, and Carmine Coppola's music holds it all together. The look on a working girl's face as a homely redneck tries to talk her down to ten bucks says it all. If you thought *Pretty Woman* was sexy stuff, you deserve to see this.

10. The recent Canadian feature *Kissed* (1996) made necrophilia look like just another misunderstood alternative lifestyle with its lush cinematography, intoxicating musical score, and cosmetically idealized couplings between its attractive young heroine and a procession of handsome beau blues. Well, forget that crap – there's nothing pretty about it. Shot in 8mm with almost no budget, the German short feature *Nekromantik* (1987) brought necrophilia to the screen more vividly than ever before, nauseating an international audience of horror

and underground film connieseurs while elevating its young director Jorg Buttgereit to instant infamy. Despite the paucity of means, Buttgereit's accomplished filmmaking abilities and undeniable (if pitch-black and fatalistic) wit lend *Nekromantik* surprising integrity, but it was calculated to offend, and that it does terribly well. It's a real stomach-turner, topped by the more polished *Nekromantik 2* (1991), which I never have made it through. When the female lead ran to the bathroom during the first five minutes to heave after peeling the clothes off her putrescent boyfriend, I asked myself, *"If she isn't enjoying this, why the hell am I watching this?"*

By the way, why are *you* reading this?

My Top Two Alien Films[68]

1. *The Man Who Fell to Earth* (1976): Director Nicolas Roeg and Paul Mayersberg adapted Walter Tevis' 1963 novel into a truly intelligent and potent 'alien film,' exploring mortality, love, sexuality, the risks of repression

---

[68] These were published in the article *"Top 10 Alien Films (as chosen by the usual gang of VMag film freaks)"* in *VMag "Alien Halloween Lucky"* #13, October 1998, pp. 20-21. *The Man Who Fell to Earth* indeed earned the #1 spot, thanks to Bill Dwight selecting the same title (*"This Glam-Rock androgyne in a silver lamé body suit turns out to be an Ubermensch and Capitalist jackal. He also manages to ooze effluvial space guy goo all over naked Candy Clark – but it comes out of his fingers because he has no personal areas!! That's the way I prefer my invaders: Give me a svelte euro-trash enigma with a flat affect any day"*), and *Earth vs. the Flying Saucers* landed in the #7 spot. That capsule writeup was published under my *nom de plume* 'Earl J. Bondgrassé'.

and expression, and even corporations – those abstract alien entities which inevitably devour the frail dreams they were built upon.

2. *Earth vs. the Flying Saucers* **(1956):** The pop ripples from Ray Harryhausen's archetypal xenophobic masterpiece continue to spread: his saucers pop up in *The 27th Day* (1957), Orson Welles' *F for Fake* (1974), The Church of the SubGenius' *Bulldada* videos, and Tim Burton's *Mars Attacks!* (1996, which borrows Ray's falling Washington Monument to flatten a pack of visiting boy scouts), and *Independence Day* (1996) is a remake.

The Halloween Dusk-to-Dawn Drive-In Theater Show[69]

I grew up in the 1960s and was driving by the 1970s. Ask me what I miss most about Halloween, and I won't hesitate: I miss Halloween Dusk-to-Dawn horror movie marathons.

My kids are lucky. We still have a couple of drive-ins in the area. Though these drive-ins are still neat, they're pale shadows of those I grew up with. Today,

---

[69] Originally published in *VMag "Alien Halloween Lucky"* #13, October 1998, pp. 14-18. I worked this up from notes I'd prepared for never-completed article I began back in 1987 on drive-in movie culture for a French horror movie fanzine that folded. This issue of *VMag* also featured my article *"The Abduction of the Abduction: The Allagash Legacy Part One"* (pp. 4-9); part two was never published. That's another story for another book…

drive-ins show the summer crop of Hollywood product fresh from the first-run mall duplexes. Family movies.

Those aren't drive-in movies.

When they come of age, my kids will never experience drive-ins as havens for biker flicks, kung-fu chopsocky, women-in-prison epics, redneck demolition derbies, and weirdo horror movies.

Drive-ins were my church as I joined the masses assembled week in and week out for unknown, unsavory, unwatchable or unforgettable obscurities like *Kill, Baby, Kill!, The Town That Dreaded Sundown, I Dismember Mama, Don't Look in the Basement, She-Devils on Wheels* and countless others.

The Halloween Dusk-to-Dawners were the best. I miss the last-minute rush to see who was driving, the ritual of packing the car with goodies and figuring out how to smuggle at least one friend in on the floor of the back seat or in the trunk. I miss the tinny sound blaring from speakers hung on the window (guaranteed to snag at least one unwary patron walking between cars and nearly bust the window glass), the occasional need to start the car to clear the fogged-up windshield, communally lift the fog bank moving in (the projectionist would interrupt the movie soundtrack to ask us to start our engines so the hot exhaust would help lift the fog!), or simply warm up (some of those Halloween nights were *cold*). I miss the between-movie stampede for the reeking restrooms, the bleary-eyed clean-up of the car floor encrusted with trash, empty bottles, and that well-stomped glaze of greasy popcorn awash in stale soda and/or beer.

But most of all, I miss the movies.

Thankfully, this Halloween you can recreate the experience in your own home with *VMag*'s handy guide to programming your own Halloween Dusk-to-Dawn Horror Movie Marathon! The trappings are up to you. The programming, though, is all-important – and with that, we can help you.

Only the first package listed below is suitable for children or younger audiences. The rest revel in the forbidden. It may take some digging and store-to-store safaris to put 'em together, but trust me, it'll be worth it. Each suggested marathon package is listed in recommended viewing order (rule of thumb: start with the oldest or slowest, always save the sickest or least coherent film for last). We've also listed substitute titles, in case you simply can't locate a recommended movie at your local video rental venue.

Family Fear-Fest: The five films selected should be acceptable to most American households. Being horror movies, they *do* feature ghosts (hence implied spiritualism), vampires, the walking dead, and killer klowns. There is a calculated escalation of gore content, too: no onscreen bloodshed in the first two; bloody fangs and stakings in the third; a potpourri of a head-bashing with a fireplace poker, briefly-seen externalized organs, a severed hand, a very nasty offscreen death, and a really scary Santa in the fourth; and *Killer Klowns* is pretty gruesome in spots (sipping blood with crazy straws from cotton-candy-cocconed human prey), but they are klowns, and it's all pretty silly with a happy ending and all. Nevertheless, some content may be objectionable.

1. *House on Haunted Hill* (1959): William Castle, master of clean-cut gimmick horror, starred Vincent Price in this archetypal haunted house movie; great fun![70]

2. *Lady in White* (1988): An earnest, heartfelt blend of Americana and traditional ghost story. The ghost of a murdered girl puts little Lukas Haas (*Witness, Mars Attacks!, Johns,* etc.) on the trail of a small-town child-killer. A moving, memorable achievement.

3. *Horror of Dracula* (1958): Christopher Lee is Dracula and Peter Cushing is Van Helsing in this handsomely mounted and performed Technicolor Hammer Films classic, building its spidery suspense to a devastating climax. Even the terrific James Bernard musical score is genuinely scary!

4. *Tales from the Crypt* (1972): Not the 1990s gore-drenched TV series/ movies, but the original 1972 Amicus Films anthology feature based on the EC horror comics, starring Ralph Richardson, Peter Cushing, and Joan Collins in five stories, each more gruesome than the last, framed by a simple but effective morality play.[71]

5. *Killer Klowns from Outer Space* (1988): An absolutely bone-headed story featuring a ton o'killer klowns, creepy and funny as can be.

Subs*: Invasion of the Body Snatchers* (the 1956 original), *The Fly* (1958 – *not* the David Cronenberg 1986 remake, which is great but hardly family-friendly), *Car-*

---

[70] See *Blur, Vol. 1*, pp. 66, and *Vol. 2*, pp. 53-54.
[71] See *Blur, Vol. 1*, pp. 162.

nival of Souls (1962 original only), *The Mummy* (1959, with Christopher Lee), *The Haunting* (1963), *The Mask* (1961, available on video in 3-D, and a great drive-in item: *"Put the Mask on* Now*!"*), *Monster Squad* (1987), *Brides of Dracula* (1960), *House of Dark Shadows* (1970), *Fright Night* (1985).

Monster Mash: Look, you don't need Halloween to stage a *Godzilla* fest. I *looooooove* giant monster movies, but let's face it, the really scary monster movies are the ones where the critters can literally creep under your skin. Here's a lineup of some of my favorite biological horrors. The first two are suitable for younger viewers, but for God's sake, get the kids to bed before the Cronenberg movie!

1. *Fiend Without a Face* **(1958):** This sf thriller from producer Richard Gordon starts like every other 1950s black-and-white clunker, but stay with it for the jaw-dropping, board-breaking, blood-splattering climactic siege of slithering, leaping brain creatures!

2. *Island of Terror* **(1966):** Another atmospheric Richard Gordon gem, starring Peter Cushing and a growing population of turtle-like unicellular monsters which feed on living bone, leaving puddles of baggy flesh behind. Bonus points for inventive special effects use of what's either canned spaghetti or some sort of Asian noodle dish. *Brrrrr!*

3. The creatures are hardly asexual in David Cronenberg's feature film debut *Shivers* (aka *They Came From Within,* **1976).** A modern high-rise apartment complex is infested with vile parasites (suggestively fecal and phallic in form) that spread like wildfire through the human population, driving one and all into orgiastic sexual frenzies. Twenty years after its release, it's still a real shocker.[72]

4. *Brain Damage* (1988): Frank Henenlotter, the maker of *Basket Case* (1982, another great entry in this lineup, if you need a substitute), offers this scatological tale of a boy and his parasite (voiced by 1950s TV horror host Zacherle) which pumps hallucinogenic chemicals directly into the lad's brain-pan in exchange for human prey.

5. *The Evil Within* (original title: *Baby Blood*, 1990): This dubbed French film starts when something bursts out of a caged tiger and slithers into the womb of a woman working with the circus. It communicates directly with its new surrogate mother, prompting her to secure the human plasma (what else?) that it needs to live. Ah, maternal devotion! This U.S. video version trims much of the gore, but it packs a punch nonetheless.[73] Unfounded rumor claims Gary Oldman dubbed the *in utero* monster's voice.

Subs: *Squirm* (1976), *Basket Case*, *Ticks* (aka *Infested*, 1993), *The Nest* (1988), John Carpenter's *The Thing* (1982), Cronenberg's *The Brood* (1979), *Possession*

---

[72] Hell, over three decades years later, it's *still* a shocker! See *Blur, Vol. 1*, pp. 99.
[73] Anchor Bay/Starz released this uncut on DVD under its original title *Baby Blood* in 2006.

(1981, with Isabel Adjani; the only U.S. video release is cut, but it's still a corker).[74]

The Classic Dusk-to-Dawn Dead Show: This needs little explanation, though *Resident Evil* game junkies owe it to themselves to catch up on these classics. The first three are by George Romero, the last two by Sam Raimi. Highly recommended, especially if you're new to tall this, and *especially* if you've never seen *any* of these movies! *What are you waiting for??!?*

1. Night of the Living Dead (1968): The one and only, the original, accept no colorized versions, substitutes, or remakes. The restored Elite Entertainment/Anchor Bay tape is recommended; beware of substandard 'public domain' dupes from Blockbuster, Star, etc., though the Hal Roach Studio and Spotlight Video versions are okay.[75]

2. *Dawn of the Dead* (1978): hey, there's got to be a morning after... the Elite/Anchor Bay 'Director's Cut' restores trimmed character bits, but the theatrical version (either Thorn/EMI or Republic releases) is the version Romero prefers himself. It's a leaner, meaner, genuinely

---

[74] Anchor Bay released *Possession* domestically on vhs and DVD in its original uncut form in 2000.

[75] Thanks to DVD, definitive editions of *Night* are easily found and affordable; I recommend the Elite Entertainment releases or recent Dimension edition, both of which are authorized releases. Still, beware variants and dupes. See *Blur, Vol. 1*, pp. 98, 102; *Vol. 3*, pg. 204; and pg. 137 of this book.

apocalyptic edit that isn't missing a nanosecond of gore.[76]

3. *Day of the Dead* (1985): Not the full-scale epic Romero intended to make, but still one of the most potent horror movies of the 1980s. The real star here is Bub (Howard Sherman), the first lovable zombie. He'll steal your heart, guaranteed. If you live in the Amherst/Sunderland MA area, pick up some Bub's BBQ to heat up for this one![77]

4. *The Evil Dead* (1981): Spam-in-a-cabin, as they say. An exhilarating, wall-to-wall welter of gore, untarnished by time.[78]

5. *Evil Dead 2: Dead by Dawn* (1987): If Tex Avery had directed a horror movie, this would be it. More a remake than a sequel, this is an ideal Halloween nightcap, especially with the remastered edition from Anchor Bay at your fingertips. *Bon Appetit!*

Subs (if you *must*): *Deathdream* aka *Dead of Night* (1974), *Messiah of Evil* (1973, aka *Dead People, Return of the Living Dead*), *Tombs of the Blind Dead* (*La Noche del Terror Ciego*, 1973), Luci Fulci's *Zombie* (1979, aka

---

[76] Anchor Bay's DVD releases offer either both edits of *Dawn*, or the alternate scenes from the European edit as a bonus. See *Blur, Vol. 1*, pp. 99-100, and pg. 137 of this volume.

[77] This is a reference to the excellent restaurant/eatery Bub's BBQ in Sunderland, Massachusetts, which is still open for business and highly recommended. Also see *Blur, Vol. 1*, pp. 102, and pg. 137 of this volume.

[78] See *Blur, Vol. 1*, pg. 100..

Zombi 2) and *The Beyond* (*E Tu Vivrai nel Terrore – L'Aldilà*, 1981), Peter Jackson's *Dead-Alive* (original title: *Braindead*, 1992), unrated version only![79]

Bloodsuckers: If you're a vampire nut, this is your night, baby. If it's to be an all-Dracula marathon, deal in a chestnut like *Scream, Blacula, Scream* (1973), *Legend of the Seven Golden Vampires* (1974, aka *7 Brothers vs. Dracula*), or *Andy Warhol's Dracula* (1974). *Interview with the Vampire* (1994) or *The Hunger* (1983) are acceptable *only* if booked with disreputable blood brothers like *The Velvet Vampire* (1971), *House of Dark Shadows* (1970) or Larry Cohen's *A Return to Salem's Lot* (1987). Lesbian vampire marathons are encouraged. Recommended lineup: *Dracula's Daughter* (1936), *The Vampire Lovers* (1970), *The Blood-Spattered Bride* (*La Novia Ensangrentada*, 1972), *Vampyres* (1974), *Daughters of Darkness* (*Les Lèvres Rouges*, 1971) However, you cannot substitute artsy crap like *Nadja* (1994)[80] for the real grue.

1. *The Fearless Vampire Killers* (1967): This is finally on tape in Roman Polanski's preferred cut, a fine, funny, and frightening summary of the tradition.

---

[79] At the time this was published, we were tough to find; all are now on DVD!

[80] Michael Almereyda's *Nadja* was a revisionist post-modern vampire film set in New York City. Though it earned solid reviews, I loathed it on first viewing, despite my affection for Almereyda's other work (*Twister*, 1989) and liking his later films (*Trance/The Eternal*, 1998; *Hamlet*, 2000, etc.).

2. *Daughters of Darkness* (*Les Lèvres Rouges*, 1971): Harry Kumel's stylish Euro-trash *vampyre lesbos* epic which *The Hunger* pirated its look and tone from. Now available in its original European cut from Anchor Bay, and highly recommended!

3. *Andy Warhol's Dracula* aka *Blood for Dracula* (1974): Udo Kier must have 'wirgin blodd' but Joe Dallesandro stays one deflowering ahead of him. Funny, gory, beautiful and tragic, but avoid the R-rated version at all costs (it even cuts Roman Polanski's delightful cameo).

4. George Romero's *Martin* (1977): Martin (John Amplas) is a shy teen blood-drinker (vampire or sexual psychopath?), an embarrassment to the family, who is shipped off to Pittsburgh to live with the patriarchal Slavic cousin who promises to snuff him if he gets out of hand. A masterpiece, restored and remastered anew on video.

5. *Near Dark* (1987): Pick up the pace with Kathryn Bigelow and Eric Red's bracing vampire road-movie, starring Lance Henriksen as surrogate father to a nomadic clutch of white-trash bloodsuckers. Great characters and some stunning horror and action sequences more than make up for the letdown last act.

6. Guillermo del Toro's *Cronos* (1993): Del Toro brings fresh blood to the form; harrowing and horrific, with a big heart.

Subs: *Thirst* (1979), *Grave of the Vampire* (1974), *Count Yorga Vampire* (1970), *The Return of Count Yor-*

ga (1971), *The Addiction* (1995), *From Dusk till Dawn* (1996, a self-contained double-feature).

Psychokillers: Leave the Michael Myers/Jason/Freddie legacies to the younger set. Alfred Hitchcock's *Psycho* (1960) is a prerequisite here. If you've never seen it, make it the first item in your Dinner-Hour-to-Dawn marathon. Assuming you've seen *Psycho* like all the rest of Western Civilization, let us proceed at dusk...

1. *The Sadist* (1962, aka *Profile of Terror*, *Sweet Baby Charlie*): This harrowing suspense-shocker based on the notorious Charlie Starkweather murder spree is finally on video thanks to Rhino. It unreels in real time, and shows what an inspired filmmaker can do with five characters, a junkyard, and a camera.

2. Paul Bartel's *Private Parts* (1972): Forget the Howard Stern title, this is the real item, a pitch-black horror comedy set in a sordid California hotel jam-packed with eccentrics, deviants and crazies – and it co-stars Chip (Stanley Livington) from *My Three Sons*!

3. *The Texas Chainsaw Massacre* (1974): Ignore the sequels, accept no substitutes. Despite the title, this is not a gorefest – there's precious little onscreen bloodshed – but it remains one of the most horrific, nerve-wracking experiences in cinema, brilliantly crafted by a mongrel pack of Texan film students.[81]

4. *Santa Sangre* (1989): An awe-inspiring, transcendental serial-killer epic by Alejandro Jodorowsky, founding

---

[81] See *Blur, Vol. 1*, pp. 98-99, 104, and pg. 138 of this volume.

father of the Midnight Movie with his blood-drenched zen-western *El Topo*.

5. *Natural Born Killers* (1994): Oliver Stone's manic meditation on our media-pumped culture of violence may have been disowned by author Quentin Tarantino, but it's still one of the keystones of the 1990s, and the ultimate psychokiller movie to date. Be sure to get the unrated director's cut.

6. *Henry: Portrait of a Serial Killer* (1986): This one's last because it cuts right to the bone. An unflinching, terrifying, believable snapshot of the real item – be prepared.[82]

Subs: *Peeping Tom* (1960), *The Honeymoon Killers* (1970), *Black Christmas* (1974), *Bay of Blood* (*Reazione a Catena*, 1971; aka *Twitch of the Death Nerve, Carnage, Last House Part II*)

Psychedelic Horrors: Bad trips, indeed! Personal discretion is advised in the accompanying use of intoxicants, herbal remedies, and/or hallucinogens while viewing. These are all wake-the-neighbors sound-system shakers – play them ***LOUD***, and Happy Trails!

1. *The Tingler* (1959): Great 1950s schlock in which Vincent Price injects 100 milligrams of LSD-25 to take the first onscreen 'trip' in the known universe. Shockshowman William Castle originally released this with

---

[82] See *Blur, Vol. 1*, pp. 101, 105, and pp. 103-106 of this volume.

buzzers installed under select theater seats to jolt screams from unwary audience members!

2. *Mantis in Lace* (1968, aka *Lila*): An acid-dosed stripper slaughters male sexist pigs in this impoverished 1960s sleazefest. Take a machete to that banana, baby!

3. Russ Meyer's *Beyond the Valley of the Dolls* (1970): Hilarious high-octane parody of the old rise-and-fall success soap, ripe with sex, violence, gender-benders and Hollywood vices. Co-scripted by Roger Ebert!

4. *Suspiria* (1977): Dario Argento's mind-twisting classic doesn't involve drugs, but it remains one of the most delirious color horror films ever made – and oh, that Goblin music.

5. *Tetsuo* (1989, aka *Tetsuo: The Iron Man*): This Japanese flesh-and-metal fusion nightmare is even more delirious and disorienting than *Suspiria*, with a pounding industrial-music score. Crank that sound system *UP!!!*

Subs: *I Drink Your Blood* (1970), *El Topo* (1970), *Brain Damage*, *Videodrome* (1983), *Altered States* (1980), *Brain Dead* (1990, not to be confused with Peter Jackson's *Braindead* aka *Dead-Alive*)

Artsy-Fartsy Trance Horror: *Warning:* This is *not* an entertainment. This is a mind-altering cinepharmaceutical fest. *Proceed at your own risk.* The goal is to arrive at an alpha-wave state between viewing and dreaming, in which you may hallucinate or dream a custom-fitted final feature of your own. And no, you cannot squeeze revisionist tripe like *Nadja* in here. It still does not qualify. Ever.[83]

1. Maya Deren's short *Meshes of the Afternoon* (1943): This is the first film on *Maya Deren, Experimental Films Vol. 1* from Mystic Fire Video. A woman, a knife, a mysterious cloaked figure, the haunting precursor to all that follows.[84]

2. *Daughter of Horror* aka *Dementia* (1955): Another woman's descent into madness in a genuinely deranged oddity that blends poverty-row urban nightmare and surrealist horror.[85]

3. Roman Polanski's *Repulsion* (1965): Catherine Deneuve is a manicurist spiraling into madness, a disintegration rendered with a terrifying, tactile clarity.

4. *Clean, Shaven* (1993): That's enough madwomen for one night, time to take a road trip with a male schizo in search of – ? More manicure mayhem, too; you've been warned.

---

[83] In the published *VMag* version, this section opened, *"Okay, this is for the Pleasant Street Video crowd. Bill and Dana will be your gurus. Trust them (after all, they* are *television stars)."* This was a regional-specific reference: *VMag* was published in Northampton, MA, home of Pleasant Street Video, where then-managers Bill Dwight and Dana Gentes were also local radio and TV personalities. Since then, Dana has become co-owner of Pleasant Street Video and Bill has his own radio show; both still work the store.

[84] See *Blur, Vol. 1*, pp. 230, 232.

[85] Note that these are two different films, *Daughter of Horror* was re-edited from *Dementia*; see *Blur, Vol. 3*, pp. 28-29.

5. David Lynch's *Eraserhead* (1977): One of the ultimate dream/nightmare/trance films of all time, starring the late Jack Nance as the put-upon Henry. Skip the oatmeal for breakfast afterwards.[86]

6. *Begotten* (1991): Real nightmare material that makes *Eraserhead* seem like a model of mainstream narrative coherence. A seated figure, splashes of – blood? A tortured nude man writhes at the feet of his cloaked tormentors; a blur of mud, blood, dung, textures, shapes, shadows: I cannot describe it. I'm still unable to shake it.[87]

Subs: *Cabinet of Dr. Caligari* (*Das Cabinet des Dr. Caligari*, 1920), Kenneth Anger's *Inauguration of the Pleasure Dome* (1954), *Carnival of Souls, Let's Scare Jessica to Death* (1971), *Trance* (*Der Fan*, 1982; available on the Canadian N.P.Y. Video label only, usually relegated to the adult room), Stanley Kubrick's *The Shining* (1980), *Twin Peaks: Fire Walk With Me* (1992)

Hey, those are my suggestions, honed by decades of drive-in and video abuse. If one of those don't suit your fancy, put your own Dusk-to-Dawn package together.

How about **Roadhog Rampages** (*Satan's Sadists*, 1969; *Werewolves on Wheels*, 1971; *Race With the Devil*, 1975; *Near Dark; Breakdown*, 1997), **Blaxploitation Boogeymen** (*Blacula*, 1972; *Blackenstein*, 1973; *Sugar Hill*, 1974 [the original on Orion Home Video]; *Dr. Black, Mr. Hyde*, 1976; *Def by Temptation*, 1990; *Tales from the Hood*, 1995), or **Killer Kids** (*The Bad Seed*,

---

[86] See *Blur, Vol. 1*, pp. 99, 104, and pg. 138 of this book.

[87] See *Blur, Vol. 1*, pp. 106, and pg. 36 of this volume.

1956; *The Other*, 1972; *The Omen*, 1976; *Devil Times Five*, 1974; *The Little Girl Who Lives Down the Lane*, 1976; *The Good Son*, 1993).

No goddamned *Nadja*, though.
Period.

Index of Reviewed Titles, *Blur*, Volumes 1-4

With few exceptions (i.e., films referred to in articles), only titles that were fully reviewed are listed in this four-volume index. The *Blur* volumes are indicated by the first number (as in 1:, indicating *Blur Volume 1*), followed by the page numbers for that respective volume relevant to the indexed title (hence, 1:220 refers to a review reprinted in *Blur Volume 1*, pg. 220). Foreign film titles are listed in their original language and primary English release title; they are also cross-referenced to their English release title, as are alternative theatrical and/or video/DVD release titles, when known. Parenthetical notation of the original release year of a film is cited only for those titles which may have been used on more than one film, or to denote originals and/or remakes reviewed; e.g., *King Kong* (1933). Film titles that begin with a number are listed first, in numerical order, before the alphabetical title listings begin, unless the number in the title was spelled out in the film's actual onscreen title (e.g., *13th Warrior, The; Thirteenth Floor, The*).

3-4 x Jûgatsu; see *Boiling Point*
6X6, see *Syracuse Tapes, The*
10 Things I Hate About You 1: 71-72
13th Warrior, The 1:185-186
15 Minutes 4:103-106
28 Days 2:208-210
1000 Augen des Dr. Mabuse, Der 2:205-208
1000 Eyes of Dr. Mabuse, The 2:205-208
3000 Miles to Graceland 4:85-87

'A' Gai Waak 2:88-89
Above the Law 4:109-110
Abre Los Ojos 1:55
Acting on Impulse 4:175
Adventures of Sebastian Cole, The 2:52
Akira 1:214, 216-217, 4:79, 163-164
All About My Mother 2:146-148, 3:79-80
All the Pretty Horses 4:27, 70
Almost Famous 3:160-163, 4:29
Along Came a Spider 4:123-124
Amantes del Círculo Polar, Los 1:74-75
American Beauty 2:61-63, 3:80-81
American Friend, The 2:128-129
American Movie 2:76-78
American Pie 1:150-151
American Psycho 2:189-203, 231, 3:62, 81
Amerikanische Freund, Der; see *American Friend, The*
Analyze This 1:39
Ancient Evil 2:237
Andy Kaufman: I'm From Hollywood 2:99-100
Andy Kaufman: Tank You Vedy Much 2:97
Andy Kaufman Special, The 2:98-99
Andy Kaufman's Midnight Special 2:99
Andy Warhol's Dracula 4:189-190
Angela's Ashes 2:148-150
Animal, The 4:131-133
Anna and the King 2:112-114, 4:43
Another Day in Paradise 1:27
Antefatto – Ecologia del Delitto; see *Bay of Blood* (1971)
Any Given Sunday 2:15, 178-180
Anywhere But Here 2:84-86
Apocalypse (1996) 1:248

Arlington Road 1:89-90
Around the Fire 2:170-173
Art of War, The 3:70-72
Astro Boy 1:215
Astronaut's Wife, The 1:196-197
At Land 1:230
Austin Powers: The Spy Who Shagged Me 1:115-116
Autumn in New York 3:104-105
Autumn Tale 1:149

Ba Mua 1:61-62
Babes in Toyland (1986) 1:155-156
Baby Blood 4:187
Bacheha-Ye Aseman; see *Children of Heaven*
Bad Lieutenant 4:175-176
Bad Timing: A Sensual Obsession 4:173
Ballad of Ramblin' Jack, The 4:53-54
Bamboozled 3:186-188
Banpaia Hantâ D; see *Vampire Hunter D*
Barbara Broadcast 4:174-175
Barefoot Gen 1:215
Bats 1:208-209, 2:237
Battlefield Earth: A Saga of the Year 3000 3:106-111
Bay of Blood (1971) 1:103, 4:138-139
Beach, The 2:155-157
Beautiful 3:150-151
Beauty and the Beast: Belle's Tales of Friendship 1:39-40
Bedazzled (1967) 3:150
Bedazzled (2000) 3: 150
BeDevil 3:155-157
Beetlejuice 2:241
Begotten 1:106, 4:36, 195-196
Being John Malkovich 2:54-56, 3:82

Bellyfruit 4:29
Besieged 1:117-118
Best in Show 4:27-28
Best Laid Plans 1:207-208
Best Man, The 1:219-220
Best of Andy Kaufman in Taxi, The 2:96
Best of Saturday Night Live, The, 1975-1980: Classics, Volume 2 2:98
Beyond, The 2:231
Beyond the Mat 2:211-216
Beyond the Valley of the Dolls 4:171, 193
Bicentennial Man 2:105-108
Big Daddy 1:106-109, 197
Big Momma's House 3:26-27
Bill and Coo (1947) 1:123
Billy Elliott 4:29
Billy Jack 1:171-172
Billy Jack Goes to Washington 1:172
Bishôjo Senshi Sêrâ Mûn; see *Sailor Moon*
Bittersweet 1:93
Black Christmas (1974) 1:162
Black Mask (1996) 1:142-143
Black Sunday (1960) 1:103, 4:137
Blade Runner 4:164
Blair Princess Project, The 1:132-133
Blair Witch 2; see *Book of Shadows: Blair Witch 2*
Blair Witch Project, The 1:76, 79-84, 88, 101, 176-177, 181, 3:202, 204
Also see: *Blair Princess Project, The; Book of Shadows: Blair Witch 2; Burkettsville 7, The; Curse of the Blair Witch; Last Broadcast, The; Massacre of the Burkittsville 7: The Blair Witch Legacy, The; Shadow of the Blair Witch*
Blanche 4:31

Blood: The Last Vampire 4:106-107
Blood Feast (1963) 1:98
Blood for Dracula, see *Andy Warhol's Dracula*
Blood Freak 1:126-127
Blood Simple 4:120-123
Bloody Murder 2:237
Bloodsucking Freaks 4:176
Blow 4:114-116
Blow Dry 4:107
Blown Away 4:176-177
Blue Streak 1:197-198
Body, The (2000) 4:80
Body Shots 1:253-254
Boiler Room 2:138-140
Boiling Point 1:93-94
Bone Collector, The 1:234-235
Book of Shadows: Blair Witch 2 3:139-141
Boom: The Sound of Eviction 4:140-142
Born Bad 1:93
Born Losers (1967) 1:171-172
Bowfinger 1:183
Boxing Helena 2:189-190
Boys and Girls 3:27-28
Boys Don't Cry 2:44-46, 3:82-83
Brain Damage 4:187
Brandon Teena Story, The 1:195-196, 2:45-46, 3:83
Breakfast of Champions 1:226-228
Bride of Frankenstein, The 1:102-103, 4:137
Bridge of Fire 4:31
Bringing Out the Dead 2:64-65
Brokedown Palace 1:201-202
Broken Vessels 1:143
Brood, The (1980) 1:104, 4:137
Buena Vista Social Club, The 1:171

Buried Treasure (1924?) 4:169-170
Burkittsville 7, The; see *Massacre of the Burkittsville 7: The Blair Witch Legacy, The*
B.U.S.T.E.D. 1:196
But I'm a Cheerleader 2:221-223
Butterfly (2000) 4:58-60

Cabinet des Dr. Caligari, Das (1919); see *Cabinet of Dr. Caligari, The*
Cabinet of Dr. Caligari, The (1919) 1:94
Café Flesh 4:177
Cal 4:164
Caligula 4:177-178
Cannibal Holocaust (1979) 1:105, 4:164-165
Can't Stop the Music 1:125
Careful 3:64-66
Carnage; see *Bay of Blood* (1971)
Carnival of Souls (1962) 1:97
Carrie 2; see *Rage: Carrie 2, The*
Cast Away 4:48-51
Castle, The (1997) 1:116-117, 4:116
Castle in the Sky; see *Laputa*
Cat People, The (1942) 1:95-96
Caveman's Valentine, The 4:75
Cecil B. DeMented 3:120-122
Celebration 1:42, 3:203
Celebrity 1:37
Cell, The (2000) 3:66-69
Chambermaid on the Titanic, The 1:72
Champagne Club, The 4:142-144
Charlie's Angels (2000) 3:167-168
Cherry Falls 3:137-139
Chicken Run 3:32, 34-35
Children of Heaven 1:51

Children of the Corn 666: Isaac's Return 1:76-77
Chocolat 4:87-90
Chôjin Densetsu Urotsukidôji; see *Urotsukidôji*
Christmas Evil (1980) 1:158-159, 162
Cider House Rules, The 2:165-166
City on Fire 4:75-76
Civil Action, A 1:33
Clean, Shaven 4:195
Come and See 1:105
Comedian Harmonists; see *Harmonists, The*
Conte d'Automne; see *Autumn Tale*
Contender, The 3:157-160
Cookie's Fortune 1:46
Corruptor, The 1:46-47, 4:43
Coven 2:78-79
Coyote Ugly 3:111-115
Cradle Will Rock 2:69-71
Crazy in Alabama 1:252-253
Crazy Stranger, The 1:72
Crimes of Passion 4:172
Crocodile (2000) 3:136
Cronos 4:191
Crouching Tiger, Hidden Dragon 4:42-46
Cruel Intentions 1:36-37
Crying Freeman 1:214
Cucaracha, La 2:150-151
Curse of Frankenstein, The 1:96-97
Curse of the Blair Witch 1:47

Dance With the Devil 1:166-167
Dancer in the Dark 3:208-214, 4:29
Daughter of Horror 3:29, 4:195
Also see: *Dementia* (1953)
Daughters of Darkness 4:190

Dawn of the Dead (1978) 1:99-100, 102, 4:137, 188
Day of the Beast, The 1:133
Day of the Dead (1985) 1:102, 4:137, 188-189
Dead Hate the Living, The 1:198-200
Dear Jesse 1:42
Decline, The 4:47
Deep Blue Sea 1:141-142, 2:231-232
Deep Crimson 1:51
Deep End of the Ocean, The 1:37-38
Delinquent (1995/2000) 3:141-149
Delivered Vacant 4:141
Dementia (1953) 3:28-29, 4:195
Demon; see *God Told Me To*
Desert Blue 1:164-165
Desert Heat 1:57
Detour (1999) 1:62
Detroit Rock City 1:151-152
Deuce Bigalow: Male Gigolo 2:114-115
Devil in Miss Jones, The 4:173
Devils, The (1971) 1:103, 4:137-138
Día de la bestia, El; see *Day of the Beast, The*
Diaboliques, Les (1955) 1:96
Dick 1:147
Dick Tracy 4:65-66
Die Hard 1:163
Diner de Cons, Le 2:60
Dinner Game, The 2:60
Dinosaur (2000) 3:119-120
Dish, The 4:116
Distant Thunder, A 1:246-247
Divine Horsemen: The Living Gods of Haiti 1:232
Divine Trash 2:135-138
Doghouse, The 4:144-146
Dogma 2:56-58

Don't Look Now (1973) 1:103-104, 4:138, 172
Doragon Bôru; see *Dragonball*
Doragon Booru Z; see *Dragonball Z*
Double Jeopardy (1999) 1:206-207
Down to Earth 4:80-81
Dr. T & The Women 3:122-123
Dracula (1931) 1:95
Dracula 2000 4:62-63
Dracula Cerca Sangue di Vergine... e Morì Di Sete!!!, see *Andy Warhol's Dracula*
Dragonball 1:217
Dragonball Z 1:217
Dragonheart: A New Beginning 2:158-162
Drainiac 4:128
Drive Me Crazy 1:235-236
Driven (1996) 4:29
Driven (2001) 4:118-120
Drop Dead Gorgeous 1:146
Dude, Where's My Car? 4:58
Dudley Do-Right 1:163-164
Dune (1984) 2:23, 3:124-130, 133-134
Dune (2000) 3:123-136

Earth vs. the Flying Saucers 4:182
Easy Rider 1:72
Eat Your Heart Out 1:43
Ed TV 1:39
Election 1:75
Element of Crime, The 1:67, 3:208-209
Emperor's New Groove, The 4:29
End of Days 2:47-49
End of the Affair 2:72-73
Enemy at the Gates 4:89-90
Enemy of the State 1:30-31

Entrapment 1:132
Entropy 1:203-204
Erin Brockovich 2:166-169
Eraserhead 1:99, 104, 4:138, 195
Ernest Scared Stupid 2:241
E.T. 2:240
Eureka 4:173
Everyone Loves Sunshine 1:196
Evil Dead, The 1:100, 4:189
Evil Dead 2: Dead by Dawn 4:189
Evil Within, The, see *Baby Blood*
Exit Wounds 4:109-111
Explorers 2:241
Existenz 1:77-78
The Exorcist (1973) 3:94-99
The Exorcist: The Version You've Never Seen Before (2000) 3:94-99
Extremely Goofy Movie, The 1:222-223
Eye of the Beholder 2:79-81
Eyes Wide Shut 1:224-226
Eyes Without a Face 1:103, 3:116-118, 4;137

Faculty, The 1:31
F.A.K.K. 2; see *Heavy Metal 2000*
Fall of the House of Usher (1960) 1:97
Family Man 3:115, 4:76-77
Fantasia 3:35, 37-38
Fantasia 2000 3:35-38
Fantasma dell'Opera, Il; see *Phantom of the Opera, The* (1998)
Fearless Vampire Killers, The 4:162, 190
Female Trouble 1:162-163
Femme de Chambre du Titanic, La; see *Chambermaid on the Titanic, The*

Festen; see *Celebration*
Fever (2000) 4:41
Fiend Without a Face 4:186
Fight Club 2:50-51, 3:83
Final Destination 2:209-210, 232
Finding Forrester 3:191-193, 4:29
Fire on the Amazon 2:121-124
For Love of the Game 2:33-35
Forbidden Zone 4:165
Forbrydelsens Element; see *Element of Crime, The*
Force Five 1:216
Forces of Nature 1:48
Four Seasons, The 1:124
Frankenweenie 2:241
Freaked 4:41
Freaks (1932) 1:95
Freaks Uncensored! 1:67
Free Money 1:78, 92-93
Freebox 4:94
Freeway 2: Confessions of a Trick Baby 1:109-110
Frequency 3:15-17
Friday the 13th (1980) 1:100
Frissons; see *Shivers* (1975)
Frogs for Snakes 1:93
From Dusk to Dawn 3: The Hangman's Daughter 1:183-184
Full Body Message 4:173

Gadjo Dilo 1:72
Galaxy Quest 2:58-59
Gekijô-ban Poketto Monsutâ: Maboroshi no Pokemon: Rugia Bakutan 3:39
General, The (1998) 1:35
General's Daughter, The 1:144-145

Geschah am Hellichten Tag, Es, see *It Happened in Broad Daylight*
Get Carter (1971) 3:151
Get Carter (2000) 3:151-152
Get Bruce! 2:49-50
Geung si Sin Sang; see *Mr. Vampire* (1985)
Ghost Dog: The Way of the Samurai 2:177-178, 3:83-84
Ghost in the Shell 1:214, 217
Giant Claw, The 1:125-126
Gift, The (2001) 4:70-72
Gigantor 1:215
Girl, Interrupted 2:102-104
Gladiator 3:40-45
Go 1:40
God Said Ha! 1:48
God Told Me To 2:96
Gods & Monsters 1:29, 4:37
Gone in 60 Seconds (1974) 3:50-51
Gone in 60 Seconds (2000) 3:50-51
Goodbye Lover 1:67-68
Good Will Hunting 3:192
Goonies 2:240
Gossip 3:29-30
Grave of the Fireflies 1:215
Great Mouse Detective, The 1:41
Green Mile, The 2:108-111
Gremlins 1:162
Grey Owl 1:209-210
Groove 3:74-75
Guyver 1:216

Hadashi no Gen; see *Barefoot Gen*
Hak Hap; see *Black Mask* (1996)
Halloween (1978) 1:100

Hamlet (2000) 3:31, 188-190, 4:29
Hands on a Hard Body 1:63
Hannibal (2001) 4:95-102
Happiness 1:28
Happy, Texas 2:42-43
Harmonists, The 1:170
Haunting, The (1999) 1:130-131, 2:237-238
Heartbeeps 2:96-97
Heavy Metal 3:47-48
Heavy Metal 2000 3:45-49
Hellraiser: Inferno 2:238
Henry: Portrait of a Serial Killer 1:101, 105, 4:103-104, 192-193
Hercules: Zero to Hero 1:39-40
Hideous Kinky 1:90
Highway Hitcher 1:133
Highwayman, The (1999) 1:228-229
Hollow Man, The 3:99-103
Home Improvement: The Series Finale 1:43
Home to Tibet 4:25-27, 29-35
Horror Chamber of Dr. Faustus; see *Eyes Without a Face*
Horror of Dracula 4:185
Hotaru no Haka; see *Grave of the Fireflies*
House of Mirth, The 4:116-117
House of Usher, The (1960); see *Fall of the House of Usher* (1960)
House on Haunted Hill, The (1959) 1:66, 2:53-54, 4:184
House on Haunted Hill, The (1999) 2:53-54, 232-233
House Without Steps, The 4:131-132
Human Traffic 3:74-75
Hunley, The 1:149
Hurlyburly 1:31-32
Hurricane, The 2:140-144

I Dream of Africa 2:180-181
I Married a Strange Person 2:76
I Spit on Your Grave 4:179
I Want You 1:114
I Was a Teenage Werewolf 1:97, 4:135-136
Idi I Smotri; see *Come and See*
Idle Hands 1:43-44
If These Walls Could Talk 2 2:223-225
Ill-Gotten Gains 1:111
Ilsa, Harem Keeper of the Oil Sheiks 4:178-179
Image of the Beast 1:246-247
In a Glass Cage 1:105-106
In Dreams 1:28
In God We Trust 2:97
In Too Deep 1:202-203
Incredible Torture Show, The, see *Bloodsucking Freaks*
Incubus (1965) 4:28-29
Inherit the Wind (1999) 1:120-121
Insignificance 4:173
Insider, The 2:35-38, 3:84-85
Inspector Gadget (1999) 1:139-141
Instinct 1:117
Invasion of the Body Snatchers (1956) 1:96, 4:185
Iron Giant, The 1:127-129
Island of Terror 4:186
It Happened in Broad Daylight 4:63-64
It's the Great Pumpkin, Charlie Brown! 2:240

Jack Bull, The 1:41-42
Jack Frost (1999) 1:110
Jack Kerouac's Road 1:51
Jacob the Liar (1975) 1:78
Jakob, der Lügner; see *Jacob the Liar* (1975)

Janguru Taitei; see *Kimba the White Lion*
Jerry Seinfeld, Live on Broadway 1:57-58
Jesus' Son 3:85-86
Jim the Rapist 4:94
Joan of Arc (1999) 1:58-59
Joe Dirt 4:108
Joe the King 1:205, 3:86-87
Jûbei Ninpûchô; see *Ninja Scroll*
Judgment 4:93
Julien Donkey-Boy 3:202-208

Kaze no Tani no Naushika; see *Nausicaä of the Valley of the Wind*
Keeping Things Whole 4:131
Kid, The (2000) 3:115-116
Kiki's Delivery Service 1:211, 217, 2:181, 184-186
Killer Klowns from Outer Space 4:185
Kimba the White Lion 1:216
King Kong (1933) 1: 102-103, 2:241, 4:137, 170
Kingdom, The (1996) 1:104-105, 3:204, 209, 213, 4:139
Kingsbury Beach 4:133
Knight's Tale, A 4:128-129
Kôkaku kidôtai; see *Ghost in the Shell*
Komodo 2:158-162
Kuraingu Furîman; see *Crying Freeman*
Kyôshoku Sôkô Guyver: Kikaku Gaihin; see *Guyver*

Lady in White 4:184-185
Lake Placid 1:172-173
Land of the Dead (2005) 1:102
Laputa 1:211, 2:186
Last Broadcast, The 1:136-138, 176-182, 3:140, 202
Last House on the Left (1972) 1:98
Last House Part II; see *Bay of Blood* (1971)

Last Seduction, The 4:175
Lathe of Heaven, The 2:199-202
Learning to Trust 4:25, 31
Leaving the Harbor 4:132
Left Behind: The Movie 1:247-249
Legend of Bagger Vance, The 3:178-181
*Legend of the Chup*acabra 1:200-201
Legend of the Overfiend; see *Urotsukidôji*
Leolo 4:179-180
Lesson Before Dying, A 1:60
*Letters from a K*iller 1:207
Lèvres Rouges, Les, see *Daughters of Darkness*
Life 1:75-76
Life is Beautiful 1:33-34, 111-113
Lik Wong; see *Riki-Oh: The Story of Ricky*
Lila, see *Mantis in Lace*
Limbo 1:131-132
Limey, The 1:241-243, 3:151
Little Monsters 2:241
Logger, The 1:133, 138-139
Lola Rennt; see *Run Lola Run*
Lorna 4:170-171
Lost and Found 1:63-64
Lost in the Funhouse: The Life and Mind of Andy Kaufman 2:97-98
Love & Basketball 2:225-227
Love Letter, The 1:132
Love of the Land, A 4:25, 31
Lovers of the Arctic Circle 1:74-75
Lung Fu Fong Wan, see *City on Fire*

Mac and Me 1:122-123
Magnolia 2:162-164, 3:87-88
Mahha GoGoGo; see *Speed R*acer

Majingâ Zetto; see *Tranzor Z*
Majo no Takkyûbin; see *Kiki's Delivery Service*
Man on the Moon 2:90-96
Man Who Fell to Earth, The 4:173, 181
Manhunter (1986) 4:96
Manos, the Hands of Fate 1:124
Mantis in Lace 4:193
Marked for Death 4:109-110
Martin 4:191
Maschera del Demonio, La; see *Black Sunday* (1960)
Massacre of the Burkittsville 7: The Blair Witch Legacy, The 1:85-88, 3:204
Master of Mosquiton: The Vampire 1:29-30
Mating Habits of the Earthbound Human, The 1:136
Matrix, The 1:51-53
Mazinger Z; see *Tranzor Z*
Me & Will 1:93
Me, Myself & Irene 3:103-104
Me, Myself, I 3:16, 115, 4:76-77
Meditation on Violence 1:233
Memento 4:111-113
Men of Honor 3:184-186
Meshes of the Afternoon 1:230, 232, 4:195
Messenger: The Story of Joan of Arc, The 2: 31-33
Metroland 1:74, 3:16
Mexican, The 4:85-86
MI2; see *Mission: Impossible 2*
Michelle Holzapfel 4:31
Mickey Blue Eyes 1:163
Midnight Special; see *Andy Kaufman's Midnight Special*
Midsummer's Night's Dream, A (1999) 1:135
Milky Way, The (1997) 1:149
Minus Man, The 2:41-42
Mission: Impossible (1996) 3:20-21

Mission: Impossible 2 3:20-26
Mission to Mars 2:202-204, 3:182-183
Mod Squad, The (1999) 1:40
Modern Vampires 1:77
Mole 4:146-147
Monkeybone 4:81-83
Mononoke Hime 1:211, 214, 217-218, 2:181-187, 3:88-89
Monster Squad 2:240
Morbid Earth 4:47
Mr. Death: The Rise and Fall of Fred A Leuchter, Jr. 2:104-105
Mr. Vampire (1985) 1:111
Mumford 2:61
Mummy, The (1999) 1:60-61
Muppets From Space 1:91-92
Murder in New Hampshire 1:201
Muse, The 1:203
Music of the Heart 2:51-52
Mustang: House of Pleasure 4:180
My Breakfast With Blassie 2:101
My Dog Skip 2:144-146
My Favorite Martian (1999) 1:53-54
My Life So Far 1:192
My Mother's Early Lovers 3:88
My Neighbor Totoro 1:211, 217, 2:181, 186
My Son the Fanatic 1:191
Mystery, Alaska 2:65-67
Mystery Men 1:174-175

Nadja 4:190, 194
Naked Man, The 1:54-55
Natural Born Killers 4:192
Nausicaä of the Valley of the Wind 1:211, 2:181, 3:133

Near Dark 4:191
Nekromantik 4:180-181
Nekromantik II 4:181
Never Been Kissed 1:90-91
New Rose Hotel 1:147-148
Nice Guys Sleep Alone 3:165-167, 170-177
Night of the Living Dead (1968) 1:98, 102, 3:204, 4:137, 188
Nightmare Before Christmas, The 2:240
Nightmare on Elm Street, A 1:100-101
Ninja Scroll 1:217
Ninth Gate, The 2:152-154
No One's a Mystery 4:93-94
Nosferatu (1921) 1:95, 4:37-40
Nothing to Fear 4:93
Notting Hill 1:113
Nutty Professor II: The Klumps, The 3:27, 51-53

O Brother Where Art Thou? 4:51-53
Ocean Park 4:147-148
October Skies 1:35
Octopus 3:53-54
Ogre, The 1:79
Omega Code, The 1:243-250
On Christmas Eve 4:47
On Deadly Ground 4:109-110
Once Upon a Time in China I, II 4:46-47
Once Upon a Time in the West 4:45
Oobieland 4:130-131
Open Your Eyes 1:55
Opening of Misty Beethoven, The 4:174-175
Orgazmo 1:28
Other Sister, The 1:44
Out for Justice 4:109-111

Out-of-Towners, The (1999) 1:55-56
Outside Providence 1:235-238
Oxygen 1:175-176

Painful Grace 4:93-94
Paradise Lost: The Child Murders at Robin Hood Hills 1:83, 86, 4:116-117
Paradise Lost 2: Revelations 4:117-118
Also see: *Last Broadcast, The*
Parasite (1997) 4:148-149
Passion of Mind 3:16, 115
Patriot, The 3:17-20
Payback 1:36, 3:152
Payday 1:67
Peeping Tom 1:66-67
Perdita Durango 1:166-167
Perfect Storm, The 3:30-31
Performance 4:172
Phantasm 1:100
Phantom of the Opera, The (1998) 1:119-120
Pikachu's Rescue Adventure 3:39
Pikachu's Vacation 1:239-240, 3:39
Pirates of Silicon Valley 1:68-69
Pitch Black 2:233-234
Plan 9 From Outer Space (1958) 1:122
Play It to the Bone 2:111-112
Pledge, The 4:63-64
Plein Soleil 2:127-128
Point Blank 3:152
Pokémon 1:211-213, 214, 218
Pokémon: The First Movie 1:238-241, 2:183
Pokémon the Movie 2000: The Power of One 3:39
Poketto monsutâ; see *Pokémon*

Poketto Monsutaa: Pikachû no Fuyu-Yasumi; see *Pikachu's Vacation*
Poketto Monsutâ: Pikachû Tankentai; see *Pikachu's Rescue Adventure*
Pollock 4:90-93
Porco Rosso 1:214
Poor Little Rich Girl, The 3:154-155
Prince of Egypt 1:48-49
Princess Mononoke 1:211, 214, 217-218, 2:181-187, 3:88-89
Private Parts (1972) 4:192
Prodigal Planet, The 1:246-247
Profile of Terror, see *Sadist, The*
Profundo Carmesí; see *Deep Crimson*
Project A 2:89-90
Psycho (1960) 1:97
Psycho (1998) 1:30, 97
Purple Noon 2:127-128
Pursuit, The 4:47
Pushing Tin 1:64-65
Python 3:136

Quills 4:29

Radio Free Steve 4:149-151
Rage: Carrie 2, The 1:69-70
Random Hearts 1:218-219
Ravenous 1:56-57
Razorblade Smile 1:51
Reazione a Catena; see *Bay of Blood* (1971)
Red Dragon 4:95-96
Red Planet 3:182-184
Red Violin, The 1:145
Regarde la Mer 4:41-42

Relatives in X,Y and Z 4:133
Remember the Titans 3:178-182, 186, 4:29
Replacements, The 3:54-55
Repulsion 4:195
Resurrection (1999) 1:114
Revelation 1:248
Rex & Red 4:156
R.I.C.C.O. 4:151-152
Ride With the Devil 2:187-188
Riffed 4:152-153
Riget; see *The Kingdom* (1996)
Riki-Oh: The Story of Ricky 1:34
Road Trip 3:69-70
Robe d'Eté, Une 4:41-42
Robotech 1:216
Rogue Trader 1:120
Rope Art 4:153-154
Route 9 1:27
Rules of Engagement 2:227-229
Run Lola Run 1:152
Runaway Bride 1:189-190
Rushmore 1:32
Rutland, U.S.A. 4:154-156

Sadist, The 4:191-192
Sailor Moon 1:217
Santa Claus (1959) 1:156-158
Santa Claus Conquers the Martians 1:127, 159-160
Santa Sangre 4:192
Sarah, Plain and Tall: Winter's End 1:149
Saving Grace (2000) 3:75-77
Saving Silverman 4:83
Say It Isn't So 4:108
Scary Movie 3:77-78

Scream 1:101, 2:129-134
Scream 3 2:129-135, 238-239
See Spot Run 4:108
See the Sea 4:41-42
Shadow of the Blair Witch; see *Massacre of the Burkittsville 7: The Blair Witch Legacy, The*
Shadow of the Vampire 4:35-40
Shaft (1971) 3:61, 63
Shaft (2000) 3:61-64
Shakespeare in Love 1:38
Shepherd 1:29
Shivers (1975) 1:99, 4:186
Shooting Blanks 4:156-157
Shrek 4:84
Shuang Long Hui; see *Twin Dragons*
Shvil Hahalav; see *Milky Way, The* (1997)
Silence of the Lambs 4:95-99, 101
Silent Night, Deadly Night (1984) 1:158, 162
Silent Partner 1:162
Simple Plan, A 1:32
Simpsons, The: Trick or Treehouse 2:234
Sindrome di Stendahl, La; see *Stendahl Syndrome, The*
Sixth Sense, The 1:250-252, 2:234, 3:89
Ski Video 4:47
Skulls, The 2:216-219
Slaves to the Underground 1:111
SLC Punk 1:70-71
Sleepy Hollow 2:81-84, 235-236
Small Wonders 2:52
Snatch 4:65-68
Snow Falling on Cedars 2:86-89, 3:90
Sometimes They Come Back... For More 1:44
Songcatcher 4:84
Sono Otoko, Kyôbô ni Tsuki; see *Violent Cop*

Sopranos, The 3:57-61
South Park: Bigger, Longer, & Uncut 1:129-130
Southie 1:44-45
Space Battleship Yamato 1:216
Space Cowboys 3:190-191
Spawn 3: The Ultimate Battle 1:40-41
Speed Racer (1967) 1:215-216
Splendor 1:132
Spy Kids 4:124-126
Sliding Doors 3:16
Spiders 3:136
Star Blazers 1:216
Star Wars: Episode 1: The Phantom Menace 2:18-30
Startup.com 4:126-128, 141
State and Main 4:54-58
Staying Alive (2001) 4:47
Stendahl Syndrome, The 1:32
Stigmata 1:220-224
Stir of Echoes, A 1:192-194, 2:236
Story of Us, The 1:204-205
Straight Story, The 2:67-69, 3:90-91
Stranger in the House; see *Black Christmas* (1974)
Stranger in the Kingdom 1:36
Stuart Little 2:46-47
Study in Choreography for Camera, A 1:233
Stuff of Dreams, The 4:25, 31
Sullivan's Travels 4:52
Summer Dress, The 4:41-42
Summer of Sam 1:152-153
Supernova 2:173-177
Superstar 2:42-43
Suspiria 4:194
Sweet and Lowdown 2:115-117
Sweet Baby Charlie, see *Sadist, The*

Sweet November 4:77
Syracuse Tapes, The 4:132

Tale of the Mummy 1:37
Talented Mr. Ripley, The 2:125-127
Tales from the Crypt (1972) 1:162, 4:185
Tales from the Gimli Hospital 3:64-66
Tarzan (1999) 1:194-195
Tarzan and His Mate 4:170
Tea With Mussolini 1:118-119
Teaching Miss Tingle 1:148-149, 2:133
Tenderness of the Wolves, The 1:79
Terror in Toyland; see *Christmas Evil* (1980)
Terror of Tiny Town, The 1:123
Terrorist, The 3:72-73
Tetsuo 4:194
Tetsuwan Atom: Uchû no Yûsha; see *Astro Boy*
Texas Chainsaw Massacre, The (1974) 1:98-99, 104, 4:138, 192
That's The Way I Like It 2:76-77
Theeviravaathi: The Terrorist 3:72-73
They Came From Within; see *Shivers* (1975)
Thief in the Night, A 1:246-247
Thing from Another World, The (1951) 1:96
Third Miracle, The 2:111, 119-121
Thirteen Days 4:72-74
Thirteenth Floor, The 1:65-66
Thomas Crown Affair, The (1968) 1:67, 168
Thomas Crown Affair, The (1999) 1:168-170
Three Kings 2:38-41, 3:91-92
Three Seasons 1:61-62
Three to Tango 2:42-43
Tian Yu; see *Xiu Xiu: The Sent-Down Girl*
Tigerland 3:193-195, 4:29

Tingler, The 4:193
Titan A.E. 3:45-49
Titus 2:189-202, 4:100
Todo Sobre Mi Madre 2:147-148
Tomcats 4:107
Tonari no Totoro; see *My Neighbor Totoro*
Topsy-Turvy 2:117-119
Toy, The (1982) 1:160-161
Toy Story 2 3:32-34, 92
Toys (1992) 1:160-161
Traffik (1989) 4:60-62
Transformers: The Movie (1986) 1:149-150
Tranzor Z 1:216
Tras el Cristal; see *In a Glass Cage*
Trekkies 1:113-114
Trial of Billy Jack, The 1:172
Tribulation 1:248
True Crime 1:38-39
Tumbleweeds 2:41-42
Turkish Delight 4:173-174
Turks Fruit, see *Turkish Delight*
Twin Dragons 1:45
Twin Falls, Idaho 1:186
Twitch of the Death Nerve; see *Bay of Blood* (1972)
Two-Lane Blacktop 1:149

U-571 2:219-221
Uchû Senkan Yamato; see *Space Battleship Yamato, Star Blazers*
Under Siege 4:109
Under Suspicion (2000) 3:105-106
Unhold, Der; see *Ogre, The*
Universal Soldier: The Return 1:163-164
Untitled, Untitled 2, Untitled 2.1 4:133

Up in the Sky: Tracey Moffat in New York 3:155-157
Urban Legends: Final Cut 3:136-137
Urban Menace 1:45-46
Urotsukidôji 1:214-215, 217

Valentine 4:77-78
Vampire Hunter D 1:216
Velocity of Gary, The 1:114
Very Eye of Night, The 1:233
Violent Cop 1:93-94
Violon Rouge, Le; see *Red Violin, The*
Virus 1:34-35
Vita è Bella, La; see *Life is Beautiful*
Vixen 4:171

Waco: The Rules of Engagement 1:34
Waiting... (2005) 3:201-202
Waiting: The Movie (2000) 3:168-170, 195-202
Waking Ned Devine 1:29, 3:76
Walk on the Moon, A 1:73
Walkabout 4:51, 172
War Zone, The 2:169-170, 3:92-93
Warriors of the Wind; see *Nausicaä of the Valley of the Wind*
Wedding Planner, The 4:64-65
What Lies Beneath 3:118-119, 4:50
When Pigs Fly 3:152-153
Whole Nine Yards, The 2:157-158
Wicked City 1:214-215
Wild, Wild West, The (1999) 1:133-135
Winter There Was Very Little Snow, The 4:132-133
Witches, The (1989) 2:240

Without Lying Down: Frances Marion and the Powerful Women of Early Hollywood 3:154-155
Wizard of Oz, The (1939) 1:79
Wo Hu Cang Long 4:42-46
Wolf Kahn: Landscape Painter 4:31
Women in Love 4:171-172
Wonder Boys, The 3:103, 163-165, 4:29
Wong Fei Hung 4:46-47
Wong Fei Hung II: Naam Yi Dong Ji Keung 4:46-47
World in Claire's Classroom, The 4:25, 31
World is Not Enough, The 2:73-76

X-Men, The 3:55-57
Xiu Xiu: The Sent-Down Girl 1:78

Y2K: Year to Kill 1:39
Yellow Submarine 1:49-51
Yeux Sans Visage, Les; see *Eyes Without a Face*
Yôjû Toshi; see *Wicked City*
You Better Watch Out; see *Christmas Evil* (1980)
You Can Count on Me 4:68-70
You Know My Name 1:164-165
Young Unknowns, The 4:147, 157-159

Zärtlichkeit der Wölfe, Die; see *Tenderness of the Wolves, The*
Zed and Two Noughts, A 1:187-188

About the Author

Stephen R. Bissette is world renowned for his 30+ years of work in comics (*Saga of the Swamp Thing, Taboo, 1963, Tyrant*, etc.) and now savors life as an artist, writer, lecturer and instructor. His latest comic story appeared in the anthology *Secrets & Lies* (Magic Inkwell Press, 2008) and he recently co-authored *Prince of Stories: The Many Worlds of Neil Gaiman* with Hank Wagner and Christopher Golden for St. Martin's Press. He presently teaches at the Center for Cartoon Studies in White River Jct., VT, and lives in Windsor, VT with his wife Marjory. Visit his website at www.srbissette.com

S.R. Bissette's Blur, Volume 1**, **2 and ***3*** are also available from Black Coat Press.

www.ingramcontent.com/pod-product-compliance
Lightning Source LLC
Chambersburg PA
CBHW022058160426
43198CB00008B/277